"*Native* is both an expansive meditation on faith through a Potawatomi lens and a powerful vision of living in relationship with divinity and in the world—one that is urgently needed today. Curtice is an essential voice."

—**Rabbi Danya Ruttenberg**, author of *Surprised by God* and *Nurture the Wow*

"It isn't very often that a book about identity—let alone dismantling white supremacy and patriarchy—reads like a poem, but that's Kaitlin. She is thoughtful decolonization set to music and wrapped in love. Her story is compelling and healing, and her path is an invitation to all of us, even as she challenges our assumptions and imaginations. I treasure each of these sacred words, rooted in her story and in the larger stories we still carry. This book can make all of us both more free and more connected to one another."

—**Sarah Bessey**, author of *Miracles and Other Reasonable Things* and *Jesus Feminist*

"There is no doubt Christianity has been the handmaiden to the destruction of Indigenous nations. *Native* is more than Kaitlin Curtice's testament. It is an indigenization of faith and, more important, a moral call not only for the Christian church but for everyone to reckon with the genocidal legacies of US settler colonialism and African slavery. As she humbly puts it, decolonization is an invitation and a gift for humankind to re-establish correct relations with each other—and the earth."

—**Nick Estes**, cofounder of The Red Nation and author of *Our History Is the Future: Standing Rock versus the Dakota Access Pipeline, and the Long Tradition of Indigenous Resistance*

"In the pages of *Native*, Kaitlin B. Curtice is a poet, professor, storyteller, and unapologetic truth-teller. This book is required reading for all those committed to learning the truth about the land we live on and the institutions we live inside of. It both stretched me and comforted me—it called me out and called me home. Curtice is a vital artist and teacher, and *Native* is her most important offering yet. It will remain on my shelf forever."

—**Glennon Doyle**, author of *Untamed*
and founder of Together Rising

"In *Native*, Curtice reminds us why our humanity matters—to explore the divine, to practice solidarity with one another, and to learn to be humble caretakers of this world. She is a brave truth-teller and a prophetic voice we need to be listening to, and *Native* is a book that will guide us toward a better future."

—**Richard Rohr, OFM**, Center for Action
and Contemplation

"In *Native*, Curtice takes the reader along as she bravely weaves together her spiritual, tribal, religious, cultural, and familial history into a cord that anchors her as she makes sense of her self, her world, and her identity. After reading this book, I may just touch a tree now and again and see it as prayer. I'm so grateful for Curtice's voice."

—**Nadia Bolz-Weber**, bestselling author, speaker,
and public theologian

NATIVE

NATIVE

IDENTITY, BELONGING, AND REDISCOVERING GOD

Kaitlin B. Curtice

Brazos Press

a division of Baker Publishing Group
Grand Rapids, Michigan

© 2020 by Kaitlin B. Curtice

Published by Brazos Press
a division of Baker Publishing Group
PO Box 6287, Grand Rapids, MI 49516-6287
www.brazospress.com

Printed in the United States of America

Library of Congress Cataloging-in-Publication Data
Names: Curtice, Kaitlin B., author.
Title: Native : identity, belonging, and rediscovering God / Kaitlin B. Curtice.
Description: Grand Rapids, Michigan : Brazos Press, a division of Baker Publishing
    Group, [2020] | Includes bibliographical references.
Identifiers: LCCN 2019038543 | ISBN 9781587434310 (paperback)
Subjects: LCSH: Curtice, Kaitlin B.—Religion. | Potawatomi Indians—Ethnic
    identity. | Indian women—Religious life—United States. | Christian women—
    Religious life—United States. | Identity (Psychology)—Religious aspects—
    Christianity. | Racism—Religious aspects—Christianity.
Classification: LCC E99.P8 C87 2020 | DDC 277.308/3092 [B]—dc23
LC record available at https://lccn.loc.gov/2019038543

ISBN 978-1-58743-489-1 (casebound)

Any poetry not otherwise attributed belongs to the author.

Published in association with Books & Such Literary Management,
52 Mission Circle, Suite 122, PMB 170, Santa Rosa, CA 95409-5370,
www.booksandsuch.com.

21 22 23 24 25 26   9 8 7 6 5

for my ancestors
and the One
they always knew

and for
Rachel Held Evans,
who believed in me
and showed me
a vision of the church
worth believing in

Contents

Introduction

WHEN YOU ARE BORN, you come into the world connected to somebody. Once that umbilical cord is severed, you become a little more distanced from the woman who birthed you, but your DNA still leaves an eternal fingerprint, your soul born to belong to this thing we call family. Sometimes those ties are broken, damaged, or met with challenges, but they are still there, asking us to look deeper, to remember how they formed us in our original state. Sometimes family becomes the people we choose, the people who move in and out of our lives to remind us that we are not alone, that we are beloved along the journey.

I was born in 1988 in an Indian hospital in Ada, Oklahoma, born to a quiet father who sang and played guitar and knew the Oklahoma red dirt we called home. I was also born a person of European descent to a mother who taught me to appreciate opera, the Eagles, and poetry in all its forms.

I was born into an America established by whiteness. While for generations, Black, Indigenous, and other people of color have struggled to be noticed, seen, and valued, we live in a nation that, from its origin, has given priority to people with white skin and

Western European ancestry. Systems of whiteness, like white supremacy itself, reward those who invest in what whiteness produces: the idea that anyone who isn't white is less-than. Whiteness both forces people into assimilation and *rewards those who stay assimilated.* Much of my life has been dictated by this, and more so because I am a white-coded Potawatomi woman. But as an adult, after I married and had children, the need to know myself outside the language and control of whiteness became an urgent matter, because to know myself is to teach my children to know who they are, to journey together toward that wholeness.

On a walk one winter day, I realized that the deep roots of my identity were coming to the surface, making themselves known in my daily thoughts, actions, and life choices. I was choosing to look back and remember, to understand, to ask the questions I had never asked before.

I began the journey backward, which, for me, was the miraculous journey forward.

As I put roots into the ground, every step I take brings more roots up to accept and welcome me in—into my heritage and into the woman I am slowly becoming, even in this very moment. Those roots are embedded in the soil of who God is and who God has always been, in the moments when I call *Papa* or *Kche Mnedo,* when I whisper in Potawatomi, *Migwetch, Mamogosnan. Thank you, Creator.*

I walk with my sons across the Chattahoochee River Trail in Atlanta where we live, and we feel the mud pulse with memory. We feel the trees tell us stories of Muscogee Creek and Cherokee people, somehow, far across time and space and blood. *They tell us stories of Natives, the original inhabitants, who walked this land and who walked with Creator.* In our Native, or Indigenous, identities all over North America, we are diverse, unique, with histories, languages, and stories that belong to us as peoples.

So I honor the truth: I am *Potawatomi,* belonging to my people, my tribe.

I belong to Turtle Island (North America), to the land that I stand on, as did my ancestors. That journey takes me deeper into myself, deeper into the heart of Mystery, the origin of everything, who knew the land's essence before any of us did. Suddenly, I see the full circle. To find our origins, even the histories of darkness that precede us, we find truth and we expose ourselves to the reality of those who walked before us and what that reality means for our lives today.

I wanted to write a book that would bring together my own reality as an Indigenous woman and the reality that I belong to the people around me, to humanity. We are responsible for the way we treat one another and the way we treat the earth, and the aim of this book is to display my journey toward what it means to be human in all of that nuance and fullness.

Every day I find intersections with other people through conversations, through the work of storytelling. And the reality is that we all began somewhere, and every person's story affects how and with whom they interact. So we remember where we come from and where it takes us. Who are you, and what were you birthed out of? Who holds you, who have you distanced yourself from, and what are you learning from those who came generations before you? In remembering these things, we recognize that believing in Creator-God-Mystery, whatever that looks like, means we believe that somewhere, at some point, God breathed. Somewhere, at some point, there was the reality of God and nothing else. So with that in mind we journey through our own stories, carrying our own experiences, living lives beyond the times of our own ancestors. We step through that reality in trust, and we find a depth of God we could not have known existed—a depth that holds us in a space where we can speak the truth to a time in which the powerful express their power through oppression and not compassion.

To know Mystery and to know ourselves is to know what it means to fight against any system that would oppress this earth we live on and every creature, human and nonhuman alike, who lives here; in knowing ourselves, we wrestle with the hard questions and seek out the hard truths. God, the Mystery, *Mamogosnan*, walks our journey and lives our history and hopes our futures just as we hope.

We start at the beginning.

We ask questions along the way.

We arrive at ourselves.

Mystery is always there.

And then we start all over again.

So I hope that in these pages, you find yourself. You may not be Native in the way that I am Native, but you belong to a people as you long for a space to know what it means to hold the realities of love, mystery, and hope. I pray that you find your own soul-origins, those origins that help you trace your steps back to those early moments of your being when you were formed and spoken to in the depths of your soul. I pray that when you journey back and find yourself there, you find the mystery of who God is and has always been. As you journey there, I am on my own journey, a Potawatomi woman's journey, and I will share with you what it means to be a woman who is a citizen of the Potawatomi Nation and descended from European people, a woman who is a Christian and yet who fights against systems of Christian colonization that do not reflect the Christ who lives in beloved unity with everyone and everything.

This book is guided by the Potawatomi flood story. I chose to use this particular story for the book because it is a story of beginning again, something that many of us have a hard time doing. We do not hold much grace for ourselves or for others, and so we do not understand what it means to start anew, to try again, to re-create, and to imagine something that has been lost. In the flood story, Creator sees that on the earth the people are causing destruction instead of sustaining peace, and after the flood, with the help of the turtle and the muskrat, the land—

Turtle Island—is created once again, a new promise for a new beginning.

Right now, we are in a flood. Right now, we are asking to begin again, to re-create and sustain what it means to be people of peace. May the flood story guide us in that pursuit.

Then may we walk into tomorrow together, side by side, with a deep and sacred knowledge burning in our bones. This is the gift of our humanity, the unfiltered essence of sacredness that we belong to and that belongs to us.

Journey with me.

We begin at the beginning.

Beginnings

Kche Mnedo flooded the earth.
Original Man sat on a tree, floating in the water, a few animals
  beside him.
They longed for land again.

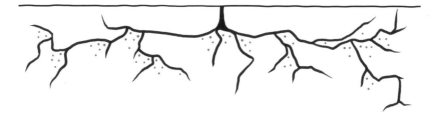

Before there was everything,
there was nothing.
But before there was nothing,
there was Something.
Something Other,
Unbound,
Beyond,
Above—
Mystery.
No one could grasp it then,
and no one can grasp it now,
not even with these
realities
coming among us
and creating
something new
day in

and
day out,
despite
our dry and weary
bones.
Because before us,
there was everything,
and before everything,
Nothing was Something,
and Something was
The Beginning,
and we are
just dust
from
Its
long,
flowing
robe.[1]

1

Land and Water

NDIGENOUS BODIES are bodies that remember. We carry stories inside us—not just stories of oppression but stories of liberation, of renewal, of survival. The sacred thing about being human is that no matter how hard we try to get rid of them, our stories *are our stories*. They are carried inside us; they hover over us; they are the tools we use to explain ourselves to one another, to connect. We cannot take away the experiences of others, but we can learn from them. We can take them and say, *What's next to make the world better? What's the next step in recognizing the sacredness of this place we've been given?*

I often wonder if we underestimate the power of epiphany. Many Indigenous cultures seek wisdom, the Great Spirit, or even the spirits of our ancestors, those who have gone before us, through visions, dreams, and prayers, through the gifts given to us in this world. This idea of longing for a vision or learning to listen to our ancestors is often lost in American society, within modern American Christianity, but what if God still speaks in dreams and visions? What if Mystery still comes to whisper to us while we are still, while we are begging for a new beginning?

Some of us might call such moments revelations, times when the lightbulb turns on and we suddenly see what we did not see before. Perhaps those revelations are spiritual, and we are just recipients of sacred whispering, heard simply because we are longing to know more.

That's how it happened for me, at least, one cold January day in Atlanta, Georgia. I currently live on land traditionally inhabited by the Muscogee Creek and Cherokee peoples. If you hike at various places throughout Georgia, you'll see tiny signs along the trails pointing to the original peoples who spent generations on the land. And in the grace that only land can give, she has held me, a Potawatomi woman, and has reminded me of who I am. After living here for a few years, our family went hiking at Sweetwater Creek, a spot of land with a long, steady stream of water surrounded by rocks and the ruins of an old cotton mill that was burned down by Union soldiers in 1864. Before that, before a history of African enslavement and years of white supremacy encroaching on this sacred land, Southeastern tribes inhabited the space, living along the shores of the creek before they were forcibly removed from Georgia during the Trail of Tears.

While hiking with my partner, Travis, and our two sons on that cold January day, I had an epiphany, that moment when the lens of my life zoomed out and I saw, truly, for the first time, what Potawatomi people once experienced—a history of forced removal from Indiana into Kansas with the Trail of Death. In that moment I was reminded of the women who walked, nursing their babies along the way (some 660 miles), just as I stood there nursing my one-year-old son in the middle of a wooded area, the trees breathing over and around us. There, standing over crinkled wet leaves, I suddenly understood what it meant to be Potawatomi. Growing up we said, "We are Potawatomi," but these words did not carry weight in our lives. We didn't name ourselves as Indigenous people or as citizens of a nation, living into our resilience. But that changed as I got older, and I have more fully come to understand that *I am Indigenous. I belong to the land, as others belong to the land.* I felt the weight of my entire body center down in my feet, as if my steps were slow motion, engaging the pulse of the earth with every movement. I suddenly understood that ancestors sometimes come to us in the oddest ways, and Mystery speaks to us when we are least expecting it. There, with one son by my side and one at my breast, I knew that the journey ahead of me would be different from the one behind me—that is how epiphanies work, after all.

We got back into the car that day and drove away from Sweetwater Creek. While Travis drove, I pulled my journal out of my bag and wrote. I wrote about those women who spoke to me. I wrote about what it might mean to embrace a part of me that had been silenced for much of my life, silenced by a culture and a country that says being Native doesn't really matter, or that all Native Americans disappeared from the face of the earth like the dinosaurs. I wrote for my own children, out of a desire for them to know who they are at the young ages of one and three, so that being Potawatomi might define something in them. I wrote about hope and about that new beginning birthed along the edge of the creek on a cold winter day, a hope that transformed the entire world right before my eyes and brought me to myself in a way that I'd never known was possible, that brought me to the reality of a God who sees and gives us the gift of seeing.

❦

We have to remember that physical places are spiritual places. We cannot disconnect the physical from the spiritual, because the spiritual is all around us, often moving like a light wind, without us even noticing. Just so, we cannot say that the earth is not speaking, teaching, leaning in to whisper something to us at any moment that we are willing to listen. Potawatomi plant ecologist and writer Robin Wall Kimmerer says, "If all the world is a commodity, how poor we grow. When all the world is a gift in motion, how wealthy we become."[1] In America we view the land as a commodity, giving it labels like "parcels," cutting it into pieces and selling it to the highest bidder. This in itself is a refusal to listen to the land. It is a refusal to hear the voices of the earth calling out, not only to one another but also to us in a spirit of kinship and belonging.

When I was young, I loved playing with grasshoppers because they became like friends. When you are a young child living in poverty, you don't have much choice but to become good friends with the creatures of the earth because they are simple, and they will always make room for you. I played with my siblings and creature friends in the red dirt of Tishomingo, Oklahoma, in the desert of New Mexico, and in the tall grasses that grew in my father's backyard in Tahlequah when he moved there after he and my mother divorced. The earth is always speaking, but over time, we lose the ability to listen. If we are lucky, we return again. If we make room inside of ourselves for childlikeness, we will make room for the ability to learn again, to be small, humble people who ask questions instead of making demands, who listen to the land instead of carving it into pieces for profit. This is the way of being Indigenous. This is the lesson learned again and again.

Lisa Dougan, president and CEO of Invisible Children, says in an essay on innocence, "Lasting change comes most assuredly when the oppressed are central agents in addressing the problems they face."[2] When it comes to the earth and the creatures around us, we should be listening. Because we, as humans, have oppressed them, we should be listening to their voices as they tell us their stories. We should pay attention to the way the birds chatter on the power lines or to their migration patterns in the winter. We should watch the ants work and remember that we are called to pick up heavy things and move them for the sake of community. We listen to water as it runs in the creek, and we listen when God whispers through tree branches on the wind. And if we desire to be people who love one another well, we have to begin with our creature kin, with the ones who crawl and slither and swim and fly, the ones who are different from us but who hold deep knowledge and incredible stories about this earth we live in.

We talk about things like climate change as if they matter, not just to us but to this earth we inhabit. As adults, we can return to the canopy of trees and rejoice in feeling small, because that is where we find the humility that grounds us in our place. We can be like children, and we can be like the dust. We cannot outrun the voice of *Segmekwe*, Mother Earth. She will always be reminding us of the dirt we were born from and the dirt we will return to. May we listen in the meantime.

◦—❀—◦

I grew up being really afraid of water, and yet we have always had a fascinating relationship. When I was very small, I waded into a pool that was too deep for my tiny body, and I fell under. I watched as the glossy surface hovered above my eyes, and I saw the outline of my sister's body come in for me. I was lifted out in time, and I was fine, but a fear was instilled in me that I couldn't shake for many years. I didn't learn to swim until I was thirteen, and after I had children, my worst nightmares were of a child's death by drowning, by currents that are too strong for my little ones to fight against.

Water can be a dangerous thing, but water is also the lifeblood of us all. It is why flood stories are so powerful and so sacred; the earth gets destroyed by water, and it gets rebuilt by that same water as it gives life to everything again. So we must hold great respect for the water, because her power is fierce, yet humble. But so often, because we do not see water as a living being, we use her, monetize her, and, in essence, lose our ability to see her as sacredly created at all.

In 2018, thirteen-year-old Autumn Peltier (from Manitoulin Island in Canada) shared her wisdom and experiences with world leaders at the United Nations General Assembly, reminding them of their responsibility to protect the water, to treat the water in a way that reflects a sacred creation, as Anishinaabe people believe. Autumn represents the future generations of our children and grandchildren who are inheriting a world that is tired (yet resilient) and has been abused for centuries. Indigenous peoples, who practice kinship with creation, can help reorient all of us to the importance of caring for the earth's water, our lifeblood.

In Western thought, fear and a mentality of scarcity distort our reality. This makes everything an enemy, instead of reminding us that all creatures of the earth, all parts of creation, have roles and abilities that can be manifested to hurt or to heal. How do we view a flood as it destroys everything we hold dear? How do we view a drought, and what is our place in it? Human beings have been destroying the earth's natural ability to make her own decisions for centuries, and she is beginning to let us know that our actions have harmful consequences.

Climate change manifests in ravaging earthquakes and tsunamis; harsh winters claim our homeless populations because our systems do not support them; insects are disappearing and crops are drying up; people go hungry in droughts that last for months on end; and we continue to poison the waters for future generations with oil pipelines. We care more about our capitalistic profit than about protecting the creatures of the earth. How do we expect *Segmekwe* to react when we treat her this way? How do we ask Creator to forgive us when there is nothing left of the earth to care for?

In Potawatomi culture, women are water protectors. To be women who are water protectors means that we know that the water that runs through our bodies is connected to the sacred waters that give sustenance to the lands around us. We lay tobacco down on the water's surface and pray. Potawatomi women in the Great Lakes region practice water ceremonies to protect the water from poison, from pollution, so that our children inherit something better. In New Zealand, the Māori tribe of Whanganui fought for the legal recognition of the Whanganui River as a person, as a part of the tribe. It's a beautiful story of overcoming colonial systems, a story of recognizing the rights of the water and of the people who care for those waters.

What if our stories of baptism in the church were rooted in that same idea of new beginnings, of personhood, just like the new beginning after a flood, after everything is drenched and overcome? What might we learn from the water? What might we learn if we listen, if we wade in—unafraid, untethered, and uninhibited—ready to become the ones we were created to become?

2

Journeying Stories

N O MATTER WHO WE ARE or where we come
from, we are people who journey. We long for
community; we long for oneness with the sa-
cred. We long to be seen and known and to see and know the
world around us. Part of the human journey is knowing what
it means to grieve, to celebrate, to get lost and be found again
and again. If it weren't so, we wouldn't be human.

And to be human is to know the journey of transformation,
to know what it means to change and become, and often to step
back into who we were before. In my life, journeying has meant
telling the truth, coming to terms with the trauma in my own
story, and leaning into the trauma and pain of others with honest
listening so that, together, we learn how to be people who walk
alongside one another in order to heal.

One rainy January afternoon a few years ago, I received an
email from a Diné woman, thanking me for my online presence:
"I have grown up in the church, but it was very much influenced
by a dated missionary and/or colonial mindset. So much so
that for much of my life I stayed away from engaging my Native

community outside of the church. I have learned the value that comes from acknowledging and learning my culture and how those teachings can affirm my faith in a way that, I believe, God intended when he created me." She continued, "I know now that I was not created a Navajo woman to conform to a majority culture way of life but to allow my heritage to shape my faith and help and encourage other Native people, especially women. However, it has been very difficult to communicate that balance of culture and faith to those who are ingrained with an Americanized or colonized view of Christianity."

A thread runs through the history of America, a thin line that connects people, places, moments, cultures, and experiences. This thread started when Columbus arrived and deemed Indigenous peoples savage and unworthy of life, a thread that continued as African peoples were enslaved and forced onto this continent. We see it today in hate crimes against people of color and religious minorities. It is a thread of whiteness, of white supremacy, that aims to erase culture, to assimilate those deemed "unworthy" of humanity. It is the greed of white men who have stolen land and committed genocide against Indigenous peoples and have for centuries suppressed our cultures. The thread of white supremacy did not end there; we continue to see its effects today, not just in KKK rallies but in everyday experiences, in systems of oppression that leave out the most vulnerable among us, that ignore and seclude Indigenous peoples and pay no mind to what justice might actually look like.

This email reflects my journeying story and the story of so many of us—people who have lived in colonized Christian circles throughout our lives and are working to *decolonize, to dismantle systems of empire and colonization around us.* Instead of living into a colonized version of Christianity in which my Indigenous self is villainized, I choose to live a life of constant *decolonizing,* the process in which my spiritual Potawatomi tradition enhances the celebration of God as liberator and the person of Jesus as a partner in that liberation. Nick Estes, citizen of the Lower Brule Sioux tribe, in his book *Our History Is the Future*, says this: "Indigenous peoples are political by default. They continue to exist as nations when they are supposed to have disappeared, and they have to fight, not only for bare survival but also for accurate representation. They incarnate the inconvenient truth that the United States was founded on genocide and the continuing theft of a continent."[1] So we send each other emails to remind each other who we are. We write books so that the truth of the Indigenous experience is not forgotten. We tell our stories so that no one forgets that we are still here and that we've always been here. In a world in which white supremacy still holds power, we remain because our words remain, just as our stories remain to tell us who we have always been, and all of that is political because our very existence works as a larger narrative of liberation, freedom, and peace.

Identity does not come to us without journey, because to learn who we are means we face difficult truths in our own lives and imagine what life might look like as those truths work themselves out inside of us. In her book, *I'm Still Here: Black Dignity in a World Made for Whiteness*, Austin Channing Brown describes the first time she attended an all-Black church with her father. "The Black church gave me the greatest sense of belonging I had ever experienced."[2] Austin, after years of growing up in a white, middle-class part of the country, discovered what it means to be a Black woman and to *journey as a Black woman*, just as my Diné friend discovered what it means to be Diné, just as I began to understand what it means to be Potawatomi as an adult. Because whiteness takes so much from us, journeying (in particular for Black people, Indigenous people, and other people of color) means that finding our way back may come in the most unexpected ways.

But the return is the key. Have you heard the story of the prodigal son, found in the New Testament (Luke 15:11–32)? In the story, a son demands to receive his inheritance from his father early, runs away from home, wastes all the money his father has given him, and returns home, weary and lonely, after he has nothing left. In the end it isn't that he ran away or that he wasted money and years of his life. The thing we notice is the journey home, the return, that open-armed father with tears streaming down his face, that son being beckoned back again. *That is the sacred power of coming home*, even if it's a home you don't recognize but long to be part of.

I did not grow up knowing that the Potawatomi people are originally from the Great Lakes region of the US. I did not know to call this land Turtle Island. I did not know that I have both a physical and a spiritual place to return to, a place that was created for me inside the breath of Mystery, just as who you are was created uniquely inside the breath of Mystery. Returning home, whether it's a physical home or spiritual home, is holy work. It is a sacred journey.

As I study the creation stories of different traditions with my sons—the Hebrew creation stories found in the Bible, or the Seven Grandfather Teachings of my Potawatomi culture alongside the teachings of the Gospels of Jesus—I find that we must learn what it means to live in an integrated way that honors the cultures and the people around us so that we can, together in solidarity, learn to go home. This means we pay attention to the horrors of cultural appropriation and that as we engage with one another and honor one another, we do not steal from one another and further continue cycles of colonization. We decolonize along the way.

The Seven Grandfather Teachings from my tribe call us back to the important and central tenets of our culture—to humility, honesty, wisdom, bravery, truth, love, and respect. In other words, through these teachings we work out the meaning of our own identity. We are taught to carry these gifts in the right way, with the right heart, to honor this earth, her creatures, and the people we encounter along the way. The deeper I lean into these teachings, the more I find the interconnectedness among all religions, all faiths, all cultures. Our work is to call each other home, to call to one another's spirits and say, "This is for you. This is what it means to be human, to love and be loved. Let's learn from one another as we go."

In living a holistic life, I engage in a holistic faith in which I cannot compartmentalize or separate the various parts of who I am or what I believe, which means journeying must include *all of me, all of us*. If we were all to engage in this way of belief for ourselves and those around us, we would see that God is truly in our midst. We would see that the Spirit is one of inclusion within our cultural boundaries but also one who calls us to so much more outside of that, to see the lives and experiences of others as beautiful and necessary aspects of our collective wholeness. *That, perhaps, is the greatest journey of all.*

Because being human and discovering the constant layering of identity is a journey, so too religion is about journeying. My experience with Christianity is a journeying story. I believe it is a story full of rights and wrongs, but for me, the origin is always the love of God—a love that has been greatly distorted by the colonizer church throughout the centuries. I believe that Christianity rooted in the love of Christ has no room for power that oppresses but advocates for power that breathes only humility, a vision of the feminine Divine, as author Mirabai Starr articulates so well in her book *Wild Mercy*.[3]

And yet, over the years, Christianity has become a thing of empire, so much so that it's difficult to tease out what is good about a religion created for following the person called Jesus, for knowing the Christ. Richard Rohr, in his beautiful book *The*

Universal Christ, says, "Our faith became a competitive theology with various parochial theories of salvation, instead of a universal cosmology inside of which all can live with an inherent dignity."[4] This is the faith I am called back to again and again, despite being brought up in a conservative evangelical faith. This, the universal Christ who, in grace and love, holds all things and all people and all creatures in that grace, is what gives me hope in this world. The universal Christ, who is not a colonizer, who does not seek after profit or create empires to rule over the poor or to oppress people, is constantly asking us to see ourselves as we fit in this sacredly created world. It is what my Potawatomi ancestors saw when they prayed to *Kche Mnedo*, to *Mamogosnan*, and is what our relatives still see when they pray today, a sacred belonging that spans time and generations and is called by many names. Today, it is what I continue to see in my own faith—not a Christianity bound by a sinner's prayer and an everyday existence ruled by gender-divided Bible studies and accountability meetings but a story of faith that's always bigger, always more inclusive, always making room at a bigger and better table full of lavish food that has already been prepared for everyone and for every created thing. *That is the journey*, ever evolving, ever creating, ever giving hope and tethering us back to ourselves and to one another.

And so, I loosely call myself a Christian. And so, I also call myself Indigenous. I am Potawatomi, constantly being called to my belonging with the love that only Creator, *Mamogosnan*, can hold, has always held, and always will hold for all of us. It is a difficult journey, and I don't know where it will lead. Years from now, I may no longer call myself a Christian, no longer engage with the church, and if so, I will still call this journey sacred as the thing that it is, the truths it has taught me, the people it has brought into my life. My faith is not a faith to be held over others or a faith that forces others into submission but an inclusive, universal faith constantly asking what the gift of Mystery truly is and how we can better care for the earth we live on, who constantly teaches us what it means to be humble. The older I get, the more I realize how wired I am for community, for relationship, for *belonging*.

Sadly, the church isn't always that place. Sadly, institutions are often run more by their rules and regulations than by a desire to accept and hold people where they are, with all that they are. So my community is the birds who chirp outside my window, wherever they are on the journey. Community is the people I've found online, who teach me something new every week, if not every day. Community is the neighborhood we live in, and it's the Oklahoma dirt that still claims me and the waters of the Great Lakes who call to me. Community is the human family and my creature kin. Community is *journey* in and of itself, and that may be one of the greatest and most challenging calls of our lives. It is the thing that sharpens us, hurts us, heals us. It is the thing that leads us home or to a new home we did not know we longed for. Community is the miracle that reminds us we are still looking, still searching, and that faith can be a partner in that journey.

3

Creation Stories

IN *AN INDIGENOUS PEOPLES' HISTORY* of the United States, Roxanne Dunbar-Ortiz writes, "Everything in US history is about the land—who oversaw and cultivated it, fished its waters, maintained its wildlife; who invaded and stole it; how it became a commodity ('real estate') broken into pieces to be bought and sold on the market."[1] Dunbar-Ortiz points to how important it is for people of the US to honor the stolen land that we live on, her stories, and the ways in which we've abused her throughout history. All the tribes of Turtle Island have creation stories. We've been asking for centuries what life was like in the beginning. Who was there and what happened when the water began to reflect a sky full of stars? In church Christians learn the Hebrew creation story; we learn about God in the beginning, how there was a sacred hovering over the waters where things were created. We learn about Adam, how he was tasked to walk through creation naming things as he pleased (Genesis 1:1–26).

I remember sitting in an adult Sunday school class at a church in Atlanta when I realized that there may be various versions of the creation story, that perhaps the story of Gilgamesh, an epic Mesopotamian poem, and the Hebrew creation story had some things in common, affected each other even. A few months later when I read the Cherokee and then the Potawatomi tales of how the earth was formed, I saw not how we are divided but how we are connected. Every time we read a story, my oldest son asks, "But is that *true*? Is that *really how it happened*?" When he asks, we always have a conversation about how we don't really know but that we can listen to and learn from the cultures of people around the world. What happened there will always be a mystery, but we can dream and imagine, theorize and wonder. We have many other stories we tell our children, stories that we've grown up with. But the reality is, it is a mystery how that very first breath brought life to that very first organism.

I'm not a scientist or a creation specialist, but I'm certainly a curious person by nature and a storyteller, and I wonder as I hear these stories how they bring us together, what space metaphor holds for all of us. Instead of holding space for Mystery, metaphors, and questions, the church gets caught up in arguing about what is and isn't literal in Hebrew Scripture, and we call it blasphemy if anyone says that the stories we read might just be a book of beautiful literature we are meant to learn from. In the book *The Manitous*, Ojibwe author Basil Johnston says that "according to the creation story, Kitchie-Manitou (the Great Spirit) had a vision, seeing, hearing, touching, tasting, smelling, sensing and knowing the universe, the world, the manitous (spirits), plants, animals, and human beings, and brought them into existence."[2] So these creation stories lead us into relationship with each other, with the world around us, with the mysteries that we cannot understand.

As I learn more about my own story, I am realizing that the bloodline of God is connected to *everything*, no matter how it was first created in the beginning. The shells on the ocean shore, the mushrooms growing in the forest, the trees stretching to the clouds, the tiniest speck of snow in the winter, and *our dust-to-dustness*—we are all connected and tethered to this sacred gift of creation.

The Potawatomi people originated in the Great Lakes region of Turtle Island. We tell stories of Skywoman, who fell to the earth from Skyworld and created land on the back of the turtle.[3] We also tell the story of Original Man, brought to the earth by *Gitchie Manitou* or *Kche Mnedo*, the Great Spirit. Original Man walked the earth and named all the creatures, living in harmony with all things in the earth. His companion was the wolf, given by Creator to help him.

In the Great Lakes region, the Potawatomi people originally lived in community with the Ottawa and Ojibwe peoples, each tribe having its own role in the community, each speaking the Algonquin-based language that varied for each of us over time. The Potawatomi, or *Bodewadmi ndaw* as we call ourselves, are *the people of the place of fire*, because we tended to the fires of the people. Over time, through migration and forced removal with the threat of European and later American invasion, our culture changed and shifted, as did our language dialects, and our stories passed from generation to generation. In 1838, over 850 Potawatomi people were forcefully removed from our home in Indiana and trekked some 660 miles to Kansas, led by general John Tipton. In his letters to Indiana governor David Wallace, Tipton says, "Everything seems to justify the belief that these unhappy people will yet learn to appreciate the interest which government has ever manifested in this affair, and teach themselves that a willing compliance to such interest, will but secure the comfort and enjoyment which for years they have failed to experience in Indiana."[4]

It seems, as with so many of the lies told by the settler US government, that these men would rather tell themselves that the Potawatomi people would be happier in a land that they had no idea how to cultivate than in the land on which their ancestors lived and thrived for centuries. It is the lie so many settlers tell: that forced removal, reservations, and oppression must be better than the primitive, backward ways *of before* for Indigenous peoples.

When the Potawatomi arrived in Kansas, they struggled as they worked hard to adapt to a new environment. They were promised houses when they arrived, and there were none. Over the first years of living in Kansas, many more Potawatomi people died. In 1861, the federal government lured some Potawatomi to Oklahoma with the promise of US citizenship upon taking land allotments. Citizen Potawatomi author Jon Boursaw writes about the Trail of Death in *Symphony in the Flint Hills Field Journal*, describing the entire process of the removal of the Potawatomi people and of the continual struggle to find a way back to our identity after arriving in Kansas and later going to Oklahoma.[5]

When Potawatomi people left Kansas for Oklahoma, they carried our origin stories with them to a land that did not know them. These stories, stories of strength and of assimilation, stories of survival and of removal, came to be a part of us. They shape our people, even today. And when we mix these stories together, we get a confused and white-dominated history. "Origin stories sometimes serve to protect us from the uncomfortable truths, like the way nostalgia for the first Thanksgiving tends to charm white folks out of confronting our ancestors' mistreatment of indigenous people," writes Rachel Held Evans.[6] She is pointing to the disparity we see in honoring the creation stories of Indigenous peoples and the origin stories we tell in the bubble of the church, or even our nation's "origin stories" of those early pioneers who made a way in an empty land. We have to be willing to be honest about all of them, to see how they overlap, how they affect one another. When I see the way the church glosses over the stories of Indigenous people, I am struck by how much weight intergenerational trauma can carry and how, if we're not careful, as Indigenous peoples we begin to embody these lies for ourselves. I feel deep within my bones what it means to be one who is removed, one who is assimilated, one whose people remain invisible. And yet, our stories will always carry us, because that is exactly what they are meant to do.

———❀———

We believe that God is one of a kind, but beyond that we can't name what or who God is exactly. *Mystery. Other. Sometimes Father, sometimes Mother, and sometimes Neither. Sometimes Friend, sometimes Challenger.* When we begin to name God, we find that God has suddenly become an image of *us,* our own cultural understandings. The conversations begin with where and how things were created, what the environment looked and smelled like, who was present, how exactly Adam got to name the animals, or why the turtle was the chosen one to create land from the shell on his back. So we rest there, and we take in the reality that whatever was used to create the world—the big bang, the little spark, a breath, a snap of the fingers, the spit and the dirt—it began in the most sacred place. Our creativity comes from the creative energy within that Mystery, and through that we have life today—a constant beginning. And that beginning leads us throughout our lives, through every adventure, every misstep, and every celebration.

Returning to our collective and personal creation narratives means asking difficult but essential questions about what we are doing on this earth. I think that trees have a lot to teach us about what it means to be kin and what it means to honor the work of creation. I'm reminded of the idea behind Peter Wohlleben's book *The Hidden Life of Trees:* that trees have social networks. Their roots are connected to one another, and they support one another through sickness and health. "Their well-being depends on their community, and when the supposedly feeble trees disappear, the others lose as well."[7] Trees demonstrate community. They understand what it means to care for one another, to care for the whole as they care for themselves. As humans, we are all connected at our root base, and in our struggle to learn what it means to be human to one another and to care for this created world, we are constantly exchanging experiences with one another, good medicine with one another, stories and relationships that are born from the deep well of God. Sometimes we forsake that sacred knowledge and instead trade violence, oppression, or fear with one another. On the one hand, healing begets healing and community begets community. On the other hand, oppression begets oppression and hate begets hate. We must choose what kind of people we want to be for the sake of *all of us*. That means that our cultures must be intermingled in those relationships, even from the very beginnings of who we are, because we are responsible to and for one another and responsible to our faith traditions, whatever they may be.

If we are responsible to and for one another, that means we are *called* to ask questions and to seek together, and to remain tethered all the while. "The task of a tribal religion, if such a religion can be said to have a task, is to determine the proper relationship that the people of the tribe must have with other living things and to develop the self-discipline within the tribal community so that man acts harmoniously with other creatures."[8] This statement from Vine Deloria Jr. in his book *God Is Red* explains a great deal of the disconnect between Indigenous belief and American Christianity as we see it today and as we have seen it throughout history. The original roots of a connectedness to creation that we find even in the New Testament, like the story of Jesus healing a blind man with spit and dirt, are lost on us in America today. We baptize people by manipulating them into faith communities in warm water in our sanctuaries because we do not understand that water is life, and that she is our guide. We do not care for this earth, and so as the earth speaks to us with warning signs such as climate change, we do not know how to respond, because we don't even see Mother Earth as a living, breathing being that we learn from. Indigenous peoples are labeled idol worshipers and animists because we have an understanding with the earth and the creatures around us that much of the white, Western church has lost. So how do non-Native people find a way to understand those roots, like the ways that Saint Francis engaged with, honored and understood the creatures around him? The answer is in the way we choose to value and care for Mother Earth, and if we truly care for her, we will honor the creation stories of all cultures, and we will do the work necessary to change things, decentering white supremacy as a threat to sustainability along the way.

My partner taught a Christian ethics class a few years ago at a small Christian college, and when they covered Genesis 1, a young man in the class commented that a main responsibility of people is to subdue the earth, as in, overpower and control "it" by any means necessary. This kind of idea, formed in the belly of toxic masculinity, is passed down generation to generation by Christians who are power hungry, who take advantage of the land and carry on the legacy of their ancestors to take what is not freely given. This idea is what settler colonialism has given us. This is how we are disconnected from the voices of the trees, of the air, of *Kche Mnedo*, the Great Spirit. May we return to our origin stories and remember.

⚬—✿—⚬

When I travel around the country to speak on my own Potawatomi identity and how the church is complicit in so much of the struggle Native peoples have faced in the past and face today, I begin every talk with a land acknowledgment. Essentially, I am naming the traditional people of the land, the original inhabitants who, in some cases, are still inhabiting these spaces and caring for the land, and if they have been forcefully removed from the land, I acknowledge that as well. I acknowledge the kindness of the land, the grace with which the land always cares for us as human beings. Land acknowledgments are a way of looking back to remember, to grieve, and to make room for difficult conversations that are still relevant today. In a way, they force us to look at the creation narratives we tell ourselves about this nation, a nation of "pull yourself up by your bootstraps" but not a nation of acknowledging the resilience of Indigenous peoples. Land acknowledgments cannot be taken lightly, and they must be done in the right way. We know that if any practice becomes rote or is done improperly, it may risk losing some of its meaning. Because land acknowledgments have been common in Canada for a while, many Canadians are talking about whether such acknowledgments are helpful or necessary anymore. It may be that they are losing their meaning, and the idea of a settler naming the original peoples of a place without really honoring or learning about those peoples dilutes an important and necessary conversation.

In the US, because we hardly use land acknowledgments, we need to consider their importance in recovering a history that has been covered up. Every time I practice a land acknowledgment, I meet people who tell me they've never heard one before, that it moved them, that it challenged them. Every time I share the Native Land website on social media and tell people to visit that map and look up who originally inhabited the land they live on, people are amazed at what they find.[9] They are embarrassed that they didn't know better. You see, it's not just knowing about the people who lived on and tended to this land, to Turtle Island, but it's also about knowing our stories, our beliefs that "education comes from the roots up."[10] Our origin stories come *from the land, because she is our teacher.* So our very connectedness to God, Sacredness, Mystery, and to our identity is in the land. Acknowledging our existence is acknowledging the existence of Mother Earth.

In 2018, we left one part of Atlanta and moved a few miles across town to a new home. In the backyard of our old house was a pine tree that I visited often. Every now and then, I'd lay tobacco at the base of the trunk and pray, because this tree reminded me of my Grandma Avis. For some reason, an ancestor visited me at this tree, when the wind shook her branches with kind laughter, dropping pine cones on my head. I'd dodge them, smiling, remembering that I am not alone. The day we moved, I went to the backyard, straight to that tree. I touched her rough skin, cried, and said goodbye to the spaces the Muscogee Creek people knew, the spaces that remind me of where I come from. I said goodbye, and when we arrived at our new home, I quietly walked along our new backyard, listening to what our new kin might have to say. These trees are different. A huge water oak sits right beside the back door, right next to our firepit. When we light that fire, when we see hawks fly across the sky and stars light up at night, we remember once again that we are not alone, that everything that has brought us to this moment, all that sacred love, has also brought the trees, the dirt, and the sky. If we believe that, we must believe that we are here to learn from one another. Land acknowledgment is about listening, it is about remembering, and it is about rejecting invisibility. It's about acknowledging the voice of creation, a voice that will continue to speak whether we listen or not. And if we are learning anything in America in the twenty-first century, it's that restoration and healing are desperately needed.

We need to begin asking what that might look like.

4

My Own Beginning

CHILDHOOD IS A STRANGE THING because it is a combination of what really happened and what we think we remember as adults. In a digital age, my children will see their childhood memories through pictures on my Instagram and Facebook feeds and in a few photo albums I've managed to fill up over the years. Much of my early childhood comes to me in snippets of memory, and if I'm lucky, I can piece together the season in which those memories took place—where we lived and who we spent our time with. We moved a lot when I was young, so sometimes it is difficult to place things, to understand things. Nonetheless, I am attempting to place my memories in some sort of order, to make sense of the things I've had a hard time remembering.

I was born in Oklahoma. I was born in an Indian hospital that was, like many around the country, built by the Indian Health Services to give medical care to American Indians and Alaska Natives. I was born nine years after my sister and seven after my brother. I grew up in a creative home, one where my siblings and I created news shows and wrote stories, a home filled with the sounds of television shows and music.

We lived in Oklahoma through my early years, visiting my Grandma Avis and my Grandmother Pauline often. The cousins, aunts, and uncles would all gather together at each other's houses and share stories that I don't really remember. But I remember the smells; I remember my senses on overload when we gathered together. I remember having a nightmare one night and crawling into bed with my Grandma Avis right before she got up to start breakfast. I remember the green, padded footstool that sat in her living room, and all the cousins who fought over it.

I remember a tub of toys that my Grandmother Pauline kept in her hallway. As soon as we walked in the door I snuck back to grab treasures from it, little colored plastic blocks that linked together with a clicking sound. I remember watching the Jerry Lewis marathon from the foldout couch that my sister and I used as a bed. I remember when my Grandmother Pauline moved to a nursing home and my mother and I went to her house to collect the last of her things. I remember the night I found out that my Grandma Avis had passed.

But I don't remember sitting and talking about the importance of being Potawatomi, or anything about identity, for that matter. I don't remember explicit words about our land or about reservations or Indian boarding schools. You see, the work of assimilation is not a one-time thing, nor is it simple. It takes on many manifestations and shows its face in many ways. When the Potawatomi people walked the Trail of Death to Kansas, assimilation was seeping in, stripping them of what they once knew. And when our ancestors moved to Oklahoma from Kansas, taking citizenship and allotment in order to survive, assimilation was asking us to become as white as we possibly could, so that we wouldn't cause a fuss, so that our Indigenous identity would be blotted out.

My father worked for the Bureau of Indian Affairs (BIA), an institution of Native police officers hired by the US government. It is problematic because it uses the institution of policing to turn

Indigenous peoples against one another, and the BIA is often seen as a barrier to tribes thriving. As a child, I did not understand this dynamic. But the BIA has always been a complicated institution. Started in the War Department of the US government by Secretary of War John Calhoun, it was created to deal with treaty and removal relations between the government and Native Americans. And yet, I simply understood that my father was a police officer. I saw the people we were surrounded with, people who were my father's friends, people who were family. As a child I did not understand that things are always more complicated than they seem.

We left Indian Territory Oklahoma and moved to New Mexico when I was young. We lived on the Pojoaque Pueblo reservation in a small trailer park with other people who I considered my friends. There were people who watched each other's kids, neighbors who took care of each other. We'd ride our bikes as fast as we could past wild dogs in the summertime, and we'd visit a store nearby that sold Pueblo artwork. We were living a reality as Native people, but we didn't talk about it. We just *were*, and my life just *was*. We moved back and forth from New Mexico to Oklahoma during the first eight years of my life, every move both traumatic and magical, losing dear friends and having the opportunity to make new ones. We always struggled financially, my parents always working to make ends meet.

When I was eight, we moved to Missouri, to a small, mostly white town with a church on every corner. I grew up in Baptist churches, but when we moved to Missouri, I experienced for the first time the unique reality of Midwest, conservative Christian culture. It wasn't long after we were there, after I turned nine, that my father left, my parents divorced, and we moved out of one duplex (only affordable with two working parents) into the most affordable duplex we could find for a single mom with three kids, which was right across the street from the education building of my primary school. My mother, a woman who has survived so much in her own life, took next step after next step to continue surviving. My sister and I shared a bunk bed and my brother had his own room across the hall. My mother converted the garage into a bedroom with a small space heater that she could use in the winter, always striving to make sure we had what we needed.

A few years later, my mother remarried. Steve, a kind pastor at a local Baptist church in our city, became my stepfather. My siblings were in college, and so it was like being an only child for the first time, a new life in the making. In the comfort of a new home, I spent my teen years living as any middle-class teenager in a small Midwest town might. It was the first time I shopped at American Eagle, or at a mall on a regular basis, for that matter. Later, I would get a holiday job at that same American Eagle, only to quit after just a month.

In those years, poverty, trailer parks, and reservations were no more, but memories stirred when I visited my dad on some weekends. Now there were Bible studies, a small public school full of teachers I got to know and love, and numerous True Love Waits rallies and other youth group events. In this season, there was barely an acknowledgment of the Potawatomi parts of myself, except for those memories that visited now and again.

Richard Rohr describes the beginnings of our life experiences as a container. The Southern Baptist church became my safety net, the building and people my community and container. They took care of me, and I took care of them. In junior high I began singing in church services. I joined the youth choir. When I was about twelve I began teaching myself how to play guitar, just like my dad had played, just to have a piece of him, memories of his honey-soft voice as he sang songs from the seventies and eighties—something that had always comforted me when I was young. I became a worship leader in the youth band and led worship for Bible studies on weekday mornings before school at a local coffee shop. My desire to care for people and build community became wrapped up in my identity as someone who led

others in the Christian faith, which later turned into a shame-
based legalism aimed at securing everyone's souls for an eternity
in heaven and shaming myself when I felt I'd failed. I valued my
friendships, but only so that I could help save souls, because
that's what being a Southern Baptist, evangelical Christian was
all about. I became a people pleaser, trying my best to never cause
a fuss but to be the best child, the best student, the best church-
goer. I followed the rules and didn't ask questions.

After leaving home during college, that container began to
crack, and I slowly stepped out of it into a new place, into a new
way of understanding my own identity and the world around me.

—•—❀—•—

Many adults I've talked to have described a coming of age with
their faith and/or identity in which they realize that what they
were given as children wasn't meant to hold up in later years. We
are all asking what the future of our identity looks like, what
our own beginnings gave us. As we ask, we begin to deconstruct
those things that were once so dear to us. We begin to let go of
things like legalism and see that though for some of us everything may have been good and safe, our faith tradition still left
out and hurt so many people who should have been welcomed.
So today, we are calling things out, things like *colonization* and
abuse. Some are coming to terms with their own white ancestors, many who were slave owners, many who supported the
toxic systems we continue to see upholding the power of white
supremacy today. These systems don't have to preach white supremacy from the pulpit, but we recognize it in even the small
ways whiteness and the American dream are elevated in our
faith spaces. From worship songs that use individualistic or even
warlike language to the spaces that we realize don't welcome so
many, we are asking what it looks like to seek justice with people
of color, within the church context. I'm asking what it looks like
to be Potawatomi *and* a Christian, when for so long I've mostly

only known what it's like to be a *white* Christian, comfortable in my own fair skin. I am asking what it looks like to retrace my steps from childhood, to gain some insight into what it means that my poverty came from generations of whiteness stealing Native identities and attempting to erase our ways of life so that there weren't words left to understand or remember what it means to be Potawatomi.

If I cannot face these questions with a community, with the people who have known me well, how do I face them in solitude? And how do we collectively work to create a better and more just future not just in the church but for everyone in all places? Professor and author Randy Woodley, in his book *Shalom and the Community of Creation*, explores the relationship between the Indigenous concept of harmony and the Hebrew concept of shalom. He also points out the church's great need to turn and listen to the voices of Indigenous peoples, not just to understand the tragedies that have taken place in America throughout history but to gain a sense of wonder and relationship with creation again. Woodley says, "We now find ourselves as children of a modern technological society divorced from creation, only allowing visitations during summer camps, nature shows on television, or through accidental encounters such as glancing at the starry sky as we cross a parking lot."[1]

We lose the ability to see things clearly when colonization sets in. We are clouded with dreams of economy and market value, and we forget that the land is still speaking, that the forgotten are still here, and that white supremacy does not have the last word. So we find ourselves trying to remember, trying to speak truth to power, and if we are loud enough, even if power doesn't necessarily listen, we are here to resist, to pressure power in the meantime. If we are loud enough, the cry of all of us, together, will bring change, and in the process we will learn more about who we are. We must begin somewhere, and learning our own story is a great place to start.

I see my childhood in two parts—the season before I turned nine and the season after. As I shared earlier, once the Potawatomi arrived in Oklahoma, we were all but assimilated into white, conservative Christian culture, which included receiving allotments of land and making deals with the government. For many of us (but not everyone), we were *set*, and that's exactly what assimilation does—it offers you a trade: your God-given identity for a chance to be *seen, to be comfortable, to fit in with ease*. For a white-coded Potawatomi girl, this was easy, because I didn't know any different. I grew up in the Baptist church even as a young child, but I was also surrounded with small glimpses of Indigenous identity. In my teenage years, I knew that I was Potawatomi, but I associated it with poverty; I absorbed messages that Indigenous people are usually alcoholics and that to belong, it is best to just maintain the status quo of white, Western America. I associated my Potawatomi identity with pain and poverty, without the knowledge of the deep traditions that led our ancestors for generations and were still, somehow, leading me. I did not know we had our own language, our own stories, our own experiences of survival. In college, I began to hunger for an identity that I knew was buried inside of me, unreachable. I did not understand that to be fully human is to own and know *all parts of myself*, instead of being told that I was one or the other.

The effects of assimilation and the loud narrative of whiteness tell us so many mistruths, like the myth that being Native isn't really important, or that there's nothing to gain from it. But the truth tells the full story. The truth looks us in the eyes and says *yes, to all that you are*. And so, in my twenties, the remnants of my divided childhood began to weave together in a holistic way, telling the entire story of who I am. I began to see a little more clearly. I began to understand, and I plunged myself into the work of learning and unlearning, of seeking and finding pieces of answers here and there, all the while learning to understand that I am Potawatomi, *and I always have been*.

~-⊛-~

Just as we remember our own creation stories, we have to remember the creation story of America, the land that was built on the backs of Indigenous and Black bodies, the America that has abused some and upheld the sure success of others. Race is a construct, as Lisa Sharon Harper writes in her book *The Very Good Gospel*: "Race is about power—in biblical terms, dominion. As a political construct, race was created by humans to determine who can exercise power within a governing structure to guide decisions regarding how to allocate resources. Racial categories do damage over time."[2]

Systems of race are set up to create hierarchy, and we must recognize that even these labels fall short. What does it mean to practice kinship, belonging, and relationship? What does it mean to have ties to our culture and our identity? Indigenous identity is not about race but about belonging. We are people who are political, constantly engaging the fight to retain our sovereignty, our identities, our languages and cultures. Structures of race do not explain kinship.

I am a descendent of Potawatomi people and European people, a descendent of both oppressed and oppressor. I come from ancestors who were both colonized and the colonizers.

So how do I reckon with this? I call myself a Christian, and yet, how do I reckon with settler colonial Christianity that is influenced by empire? We are taught about who Jesus is, but in Western Christianity we are taught a diluted, whitewashed version. Settler colonial Christianity puts itself at the center of everything as the sole power, and evangelism becomes a tool used to erase other cultures and religions from the people whom Christians are meant to serve. Settler colonial Christianity is a religion that takes, that demeans the earth and the oppressed, and that holds people in these systems without regard for how Jesus treated people. So to be part of a colonizing religion, I have to constantly

ask, Who am I following? The empirical religion born of men
who wanted and still want to rule the world in their own image,
or something different? I am a woman, but what does it mean to
embody that in a toxic, patriarchal society and church system?

It means I listen to the voice that has been silenced. It means
I give room for colonization to be uprooted in my life and in the
life of my family. It means we have regular conversations about
our own white privilege in the spaces we inhabit.

I belong to the Oklahoma dirt that I was born on, but like the
umbilical cord that connects mother and child at birth, my connection to Potawatomi land goes back to another beginning for
my people in the Great Lakes region of the US. I dream not only
of the red dirt of Oklahoma but of tapping maple trees and growing wild rice in Michigan. I dream of ceremony and traditional
Potawatomi prayers. I dream of a new beginning for myself and
for my children—a beginning that has never really been new at
all. To begin at our own beginnings, we ask questions about this
created world, about our place in it, about what it means to *belong*.
We think about how we are called to care for one another. Then
we take the constant lessons we are learning and we apply them
to our faith, to our traditions, and to our relationships with one
another as we begin to seek out the nature of wholeness in our
midst. In that space, we ask what part identity and culture have
to play as we read the creation stories and learn from wisdom
traditions, as we ask how to incorporate the lessons and values
from those traditions into our lives today without appropriating
them. They form us, whether we realize it or not, and they form
our ideas of one another.

When *Black Panther*—a superhero movie that takes place
in Wakanda, a utopian, highly technological African state that
has never been colonized—came out in 2018, people flocked to
the movie theater for an experience of Blackness that many of
my Black friends said they were hungry for. To see a land of
celebrated Blackness, a land yet to be colonized, gave an image

to people across the world, an image that challenges the racial constructs we've set up to decide who is more or less than. We need more stories like those of Wakanda. We need more stories that celebrate who we are instead of making us into the "other."

Once we open our imaginations to the reality of the value that Indigenous and Black people carry, it will inevitably create a different future for all of us, a future that I believe God envisioned in the very beginning, a vision of a world full of fierce love and sacred belonging.

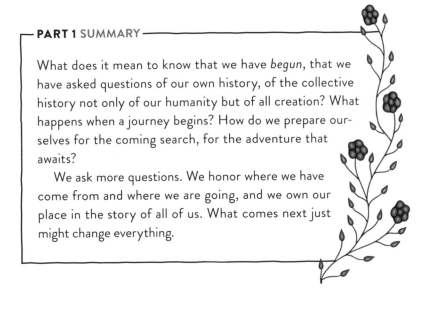

PART 1 SUMMARY

What does it mean to know that we have *begun*, that we have asked questions of our own history, of the collective history not only of our humanity but of all creation? What happens when a journey begins? How do we prepare ourselves for the coming search, for the adventure that awaits?

We ask more questions. We honor where we have come from and where we are going, and we own our place in the story of all of us. What comes next just might change everything.

Searching for Meaning

Original Man dived down into the water to search for earth, but he couldn't find any.

So duck dived down and searched. Still nothing.

Loon searched, but came up empty.

Finally, muskrat said that he would do it, that he would get the dirt they needed to begin again.

No one really believed he could do it, but they let him try.

Muskrat dove into the water and went deeper, deeper, deeper . . .

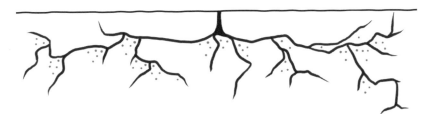

Every now and then,
we should hear the coffee mug clank
as we set it back down on the
glass tabletop,
because there is nothing
to distract us
from
its
presence.

We should listen
for the creaking beams
of an old house,
whose bones ache with a kind of
architectural osteoporosis.
We should listen for her groans
because they remind us
that
history
lives.

And more often than not,
the hummingbirds should get
our full attention,
because they teach us what it means
to gulp the nectar of life.
They teach us to remember
that we, too, are small, thirsty things,
looking for the river to drink from,
or, at least,

a

refreshing
fountain.

5

The Problem of Whiteness

> [President Trump] is kind of the new incarnation of Andrew Jackson. Bad president for Indian people, bad president for everybody. . . . We don't have a lot of experience with great presidents.
>
> Winona LaDuke, Democracy Now! interview

O N EARTH DAY IN 2018, it rained most of the afternoon. During a lull in the dreary weather, I went outside to check on our garden. I had planted seeds a month earlier, and nothing came up, probably because the soil had hardened during an earlier weeklong storm. In order for my tomatoes, broccoli, and sugar snap peas to grow, I needed to till up the ground again, add some compost, and pull up weeds.

I grabbed my hand tiller, one of those that you stand on, push into the ground, and turn into the dirt so that it pulls up weeds along with it. I stood at the corner of the garden, hitting the same patch of ground over and over again, and eventually mumbled to myself, "There's something going on down there." I knew then and there that the dirt represented deeper issues that were preventing growth.

We've been spending so much time in the Trump era trying to dig up weeds, to figure out what's gone wrong with colonial, white Christianity, but it won't do us any good to pull up only the weeds we can see if we don't get down to those roots that have dug their spindly, tight fingers into the dirt of our very foundations.

White supremacy is that root. It is the core of all those fingers, way down deep where we can't see, and its tendrils reach up through our good soil and damage whatever fruit we've tried to cultivate all these years, all the work we've done. In November 2018, an unprecedented number of women of color were elected to Congress, including the first Indigenous women ever elected, Deb Haaland (Laguna Pueblo) and Sharice Davids (Ho-Chunk). In the midst of pulling up roots, America is stepping into the light of calling out white supremacy for what it is, and many people are seen as beacons of that hope, of a change in the very halls of government. Those who are in power must continue to do the work of decolonizing, but they cannot do it alone, and they must be held accountable. And it cannot stop there. Many of our white American churches have held up white supremacy as a shining model of Christianity, and this egregious evil must be named as well.

In Baptist Sunday school growing up, I took in every Hebrew Bible story and New Testament parable as truth, because they were life to me. I asked no questions, because it was believed that the men and women in my churches knew best. But what was happening under the surface was a slow and steady assimilation into Western American Christianity—what I now see as the mix of empire and God that permeates so many white American churches. The problem with the white evangelical church is that assimilation is subtle; when you walk through that sanctuary door, the assumption is that you participate, you oblige, and you don't cause a fuss. What I learned in my church growing up was how to be a devout evangelical, but I was also being taught that for my identity to matter, I must assimilate and take on the American dream as best I could. My life became about pleasing an Americanized God who really cannot be pleased.

We remember that stories of Christianity and imperialism, of power and control, have been present all over the world as Christianity became a religion that benefited those at the top more than those at the bottom—rather than a religion that encouraged people to follow the lifestyle and teachings of Jesus. Instead of doing good in the world, many Christians used the name of God to actually create those hierarchies.

We remember that people have been oppressed by the church, oppressed in the name of Jesus, and told that they cannot possibly know God in the way they were born to know God, and that it has resulted in splits and fractures in the world.

We remember, and we begin to ask questions. Many of us ask whether God is really a God who is white, a God who is a patriarchal slave driver. *How can this be God? How can the church reconcile this, years later, when it feels like the church itself is imploding?*

How can the white American church, with a history of complicity and abuse toward Indigenous peoples, ask any questions about the nature of God if we cannot ask ourselves to take an honest look at our own intentions? As Vine Deloria Jr. says in his book *God Is Red*, "Instead of working toward the Kingdom of God on Earth, history becomes the story of a particular race fulfilling its manifest destiny."[1] Whiteness is a culture that requires the erasure of all others, considering them less-than. It is believing in that well-known metaphor of a melting pot that we so love to hold on to in America, but erasing the value of the lives of the "other" within the narrative and in the process presenting the idea of assimilation as virtue. But really, assimilation is about power, power that puts shackles on Black people, Indigenous people, and other people of color.

Recently I sat at a dinner table with my friend Jacqui and a group of women from mixed backgrounds culturally, racially, and ethnically. In that space, Jacqui reminded us that we must own our identities for the sake of *all of us*, for the sake of our white kin. Because, at the end of the day, whiteness doesn't truly give anyone *anything*. It is a culture of taking and erasing, and we must learn from our mistakes and actively work toward healing.

The church is a searching being, because the people within it are searching. But who are we searching for? How much are we searching? When we search, do we fear who or what we will find?

The more *we* define God as an old, white man with a gavel, the more we create a society based around that idea, around the hate in that metaphor, and eventually, it bleeds into everything we do and believe. As Richard Twiss, member of the Sicangu Lakota Oyate tribe, once said, "When the heart is flooded with racial, cultural, ideological or denominational strife, there is little room in the heart to hold love, honor, respect and admiration for those who are different from us."[2] Over time, it leaves us with a church culture and identity so blended in with whiteness that we have learned to no longer value those who wish to decolonize, to separate themselves from the work of assimilation. In other words, the church has *a lot of work to do*.

❧—✿—❧

The problem of a white God stretches into so many parts of our culture, even into the race politics of DNA tests, which have been used by people to "prove" their Native American identity when they have no real ties to an Indigenous community. In 2018 Elizabeth Warren came out with her DNA test results as a way to fight back against Trump's claims that she's not really Native, and as a result there was an uproar within some Indigenous communities, especially from people within the Cherokee tribe Warren claimed to be connected to. Because tribes have fought so hard to have sovereign rights, this battle, simplistic at best, between Trump and Warren over whether she should be called *Pocahontas* or not, came down to a test that says nothing of kinship within tribes. Elizabeth Warren *is not claimed by the Cherokee people*, and yet she made a public effort to stake a claim on their identity for herself. Test results do not equate kinship with an Indigenous community, yet Americans flock to DNA tests to give them answers to this question: *Am I Native?*

Daniel Heath Justice, an academic writer and member of the Cherokee nation living in Canada, explains it like this: "The simple fact of DNA relation isn't actually kinship, or at least not entirely; to be a *good* relative, to be fully *kin*, we must put that relatedness into thoughtful and respectful practice, individually and collectively, and take up our responsibilities to one another and to the world of which we're a part."[3]

Despite all the ways she's working to be an ally and spokesperson for Indigenous peoples, Warren nonetheless is breaking the very laws of kinship and belonging. By taking a DNA test to say that she's *part Native American*, she is essentially telling all tribes, especially the Cherokee people, that stories told within non-Native families about that "one Native relative" aren't problematic and that Native identity can be determined by a simple test. Kim Tallbear, associate professor of Native studies at the University of Alberta, has an incredible book on this topic. In *Native American DNA*, Tallbear critiques DNA test companies and the implications of these tests for Native communities. She writes, "Race politics over the centuries in both Europe and the US have conditioned our experiences and opportunities, including the federal-tribal relationship. They have impinged upon our ability as indigenous peoples to exercise self-governance."[4] This is exactly what Warren's experiment in DNA testing has done: solidify the idea that anyone can take a test and claim to be racially "Native," while erasing the actual cultural identity of Indigenous peoples. In the fight between Christian conservatives who side with Trump and Christian liberals who side with Warren, Native peoples who oppose them are left in the middle, traumatized over and over again, mocked for the very identities that we hold to be sacred in our own cultures.

In early 2019, right after Warren held a rally to announce her run for the presidency, Trump tweeted at her, saying, "Today Elizabeth Warren, sometimes referred to by me as Pocahontas, joined the race for President. Will she run as our first Native American presidential candidate, or has she decided that after 32 years, this is not playing so well anymore? See you on the campaign TRAIL, Liz!"[5] This tweet, mocking the Trail of Tears—the forced removal of Cherokee people (and other Southeastern tribes) from their homelands—left Cherokee people the target for racist hate speech and toxic stereotypes that have been around for centuries, now exacerbated by this battle between a woman who claimed Native identity and a racist president who doesn't care who he harms. It is important to remember that Indigenous voices are not homogenous, and Indigenous voices should be listened to on all sides of issues like these. If we want to talk about these issues and center Indigenous experiences, *both sides* of the political spectrum are guilty of using and abusing Indigenous identity for their own gain. We must address this reality in our political and religious spaces, because if we don't, white supremacy will continue to hold power. My hope is that Warren will apologize in the right way by speaking about the settler narratives that often erase Indigenous identity and that she will then build long-lasting relationships with Indigenous peoples, because we need to see more stories of solidarity in our midst, of power to overcome systems of oppression and erasure.

White supremacy within our politics and within our churches should be addressed on a number of levels, but if we cannot admit that we have a problem in the first place, nothing will ever change. DNA tests will come out, people will lay claim over a culture that they have no part in, and our ideas of true kinship and belonging will be made into a mockery—and I believe all of this greatly grieves the heart of God and destroys the sacred love with which we should respond to each other. Our political arenas and our churches are spaces in which we largely ignore the oppression of Indigenous peoples, people of color, women, LGBTQ+ folks, and disabled people, because we see only that individualist God who looks at our sins and yet ignores the bigger picture of what we've created and have been complicit in creating. May the problems of whiteness we have created move us to create a better future for those who come after us.

~—❀—~

"Many white people would rather do something to address the symptoms we can see than acknowledge our original sin. . . . If we are honest with ourselves, we carry the wounds of white supremacy in our bodies."[6] These words by Jonathan Wilson-Hartgrove epitomize the problem of whiteness in America. Many Christians who are embedded in white supremacist systems within the church, when confronted with those systems of racism, would rather give away money and look at it from a distance, or, as has often been done, send in missionaries to fix the problem.

Being white-coded, both a descendent of European people and a citizen of the Potawatomi nation, means that though I belong to the Potawatomi, I am also responsible for the ways in which I have participated in the work of white supremacy. Growing up in church, I went on several short-term mission trips, and I showed up at church once a week to participate in F.A.I.T.H. visits, which were door-to-door evangelism to people who attended our church once or twice, just to see if they needed saving and, possibly, community. While our intentions were to care for people, to *love* people, we instead created systems of colonization through our evangelism and missional programs.

This problem of centering whiteness within Christianity has resulted in the invasion and erasure of cultures all over the world. In 2018 a young man named John Allen Chau traveled to the Sentinelese Islands to Indigenous people living right outside India. Chau, as he described it, was there to save them, because of his deep love for them through Jesus. Chau ignored years of legal protection placed on the Sentinelese peoples, who have remained connected to their own culture and traditions without contact by outsiders and who wish to remain as they have always been. Giving Indigenous peoples the right to be left alone was trumped by one missionary who wanted to "share the love of Christ," and in doing so, he lost his life to a people who were protecting themselves once again from the outside world.

What happens when white supremacy taints our Christianity so much that we would rather scream the love of God over someone than honor and respect their rights to live peacefully within the communities they have created and maintained for generations? If Christianity is able to de-center itself enough to see that the imprint of Sacred Mystery already belongs all over the earth, to all peoples, it would change the way we treat our human *and nonhuman* kin.

Instead, the church jumps to addressing a symptom, which often results in missional projects that do not honor the cultures of other people, perpetuating cycles of colonization all over the world. There is certainly a right way to engage with people of other cultures and faiths, and we must see that there is a very real problem of continual colonization. America was founded in part on the image of the "just missionary" who came to save the "heathen," and flowing out of that was the inability to see humanity in Indigenous peoples all over the world, including Indigenous Africans stolen from their homelands and shipped to the US to be enslaved.

Conversations around whiteness can be very difficult, but it is imperative that we speak openly and honestly with one another.

While I believe we should be gentle with one another, we must speak the truth, and the truth is that our church systems, social systems, and our government systems run with white supremacy coursing through their veins. Until we are honest about that, nothing in the church is going to change. Individuals may find ways to *decolonize*, to return to the space in which all creatures and peoples of this earth are honored for who they are, but within our institutions, we cannot fix what we won't admit is broken.

The time is now, and the work cannot fall only on Black people, Indigenous people, and people of color. Breaking down systems of toxic patriarchy cannot fall only on women. Breaking down systems of homophobia cannot fall only on our LGBTQ+, two-spirit, and nonbinary kin. Breaking down systems of ableism cannot fall only to disabled people. Breaking down systems of destructive mental-health practices and stigmas cannot fall only on those who are on a journey with mental health. Breaking down systems of terrorizing the earth cannot be the work of Indigenous peoples alone. We must work together, across every divide, and the church must be willing to step into really difficult conversations for the sake of a better future for *all things and everyone*. Maybe that begins with recognizing that all created things are truly sacred in their beginnings, and maybe then we can truly begin to dismantle systems of oppression.

6

Stereotypes and Survival

UPON ARRIVING AT THE AIRPORT for a speaking event at Duke University in North Carolina, I was picked up by a woman who drove me to campus. She was an immigrant who had lived in America for years. And as soon as I told her I am Native, she said, "Look at those cheekbones! You're like Pocahontas," and then chuckled to herself for a few seconds. I smiled awkwardly and looked out my window, remembering once again that this is exactly what America sees when they look at Native women, if they choose to see us at all. What spoke to me more in that moment wasn't disgust for this woman's comment, but disgust for the fact that this is what she learned of Native people from the years she had lived in the US. Of any stories told, the stories she'd heard were most likely the ones that romanticize old westerns, make us savages, paint us as cartoons in a Disney movie, or sexualize Indigenous women's bodies. Most of America believes there are certain features that make someone *look* "Native," despite the fact that features greatly vary from person to person, and there is no uniform "Native" look. The truth is, so many people have a romanticized version of Native people, a New Age imagery in which we are sitting with crystals, chanting over a fire outside a tipi, or spending days in a sweat lodge praying, always with braided hair and wearing buckskin with fringes. Every one of us is presented as an old sage or a warrior, perpetuating the stereotypes built over the reality of our diverse societies and cultures. When we forget that there is diversity among peoples, we begin to create patterns and stereotypes, to expect people who come from certain cultures to *look* or *act* a certain way, which creates the perfect soil for growing discrimination and microaggressions.

When I was a young, summer-tanned girl, I went to the Citizen Potawatomi Nation tribal headquarters in Shawnee, Oklahoma, with my dad to receive my tribal rolls card, the card that shows I am an enrolled citizen of our nation. I dressed up that day, my chin-length hair decorated with butterfly clips and my ears with shiny studded earrings. I still have that card, and when I look at it now, I think how odd it is that in this world there are people groups that have to carry cards to show who they are, to prove their humanity. I belong to that card, just as I belong to my people. Not all tribes are federally recognized, and I have many friends who are not citizens or members of their tribe, yet they still fully participate in their identity as Indigenous people. They still know what it means to *belong*, whether it is recognized by society or not.

I've carried that card all these years, on every move from New Mexico to Missouri, Arkansas to Georgia. I kept that card in my wallet or in a safe drawer at home, a distant reminder of who I was but in ways I didn't always understand. I went to our tribe's headquarters in the summer of 2017, and they gave me a new card. This time, the picture was a little more blurred than last time. I still have the dark hair and the dark eyes but there are no butterfly clips in sight.

A few years ago, on the first Saturday in November, our family attended a powwow in our city. When we returned home,

I couldn't find my wallet, which held both my tribal ID from childhood and the new ID I had gotten a few months earlier. I didn't care about the credit cards in the wallet; all I wanted was that ID, that thing that tied me to my identity in a particularly important way. I felt lost without it, and I was sure I'd left it in the grass or somewhere on the pavement where we'd parked. Later I found it behind some furniture in my bedroom. I opened it and came face to face with my own reflection, one card with a picture of a little girl working out her identity only to have it silenced and another card with a picture of a woman who is working to reclaim it every day. The reality is, that card is *not* my entire identity. But it is a symbol of identity, a tangible thing that reminds me every day of my belonging.

Whiteness, in more ways than we can comprehend, erases identity. I have to hold the reality of my white privilege as a white-coded Indigenous woman, and I have to use that privilege in ways that honor the Indigenous experience in all its complexities; this is part of my particular journey with survival and speaks to my own felt necessity to decolonize my life wherever I can. I watch as people often grow uncomfortable and uneasy because they don't know how to react, how to engage, how to respond when I tell them that I am Potawatomi. Because Indigenous culture, though it has been here all this time, is foreign and unknown to so many Americans, it is often seen as either exotic or threatening, especially within educational systems, politics, and the church. If I am not comfortable in my own skin, with the knowns and the unknowns of this journey, with the body that defines me and the past that stays with me, I will fail in the search for what it means to be Potawatomi. As humans, we are simply asked to walk in the mystery of our identities one day at a time, one step at a time, one question at a time. We are simply asked to know and be known with the whole of creation and our relatives in humanity. But to do that, we have to accept, challenge, and process who we are along the way.

When I was in fourth grade, I chopped off all of my hair; we bought tiny koi fish bobby pins that I used to pin back my bangs. I remember sitting in the car at the gas station, hoping I'd still be beautiful with all my hair chopped off. I was called a boy by some of the kids at school, but I loved having short hair because it felt right for me, fitting to who I was becoming. I dreamt for a long time when I was younger about wearing my hair in one long, dark brown braid, but instead it stayed short for years. As an adult, I learned that women in our tribe traditionally wore their hair that way—one long braid straight down the back—and that image meant something holy to me, a tethering to who I am and have always been.

When I was pregnant with my second son and had been growing my hair back out for a while, I took the shearers out of the bathroom and handed them to my partner, Travis. "Shave my head," I said. It was the gut-drop akin to a roller-coaster ride, and I didn't look in the mirror until it was all gone, just my little head with a short layer of brown peach fuzz all over it. I kept it that way for over a year, because it was calling something out of me, a new woman with a confidence that I hadn't known before, a journey into seeking and understanding identity.

It seems simplistic to talk about identity through hair, but sometimes, who we are is hidden. It's forgotten, like closed-off and uncharted territory, waiting within us to be examined and explored. Sometimes even a haircut reveals those hidden spaces, reminds us of who we are and who we are longing to become. For me, understanding my identity has been a means of survival, of knowing that the trauma I've endured in my life doesn't have the last word, but it can compel me to do the work I do in the world.

That vision of a woman with a long braid, a vision of myself that I had never really known, wouldn't let go of me but continued to tug me toward a new life season, because even hair means something, whether we acknowledge that or not. Throughout history in the US, and even today, Indigenous children who have braids are told to cut their hair or are punished for having long hair in the first place. In 2018 a teacher in New Mexico cut three inches off one student's braid and called another student a "bloody Indian." After the assault, students protested and eventually the teacher was removed from her job.[1] With all the other things Indigenous peoples deal with, we shouldn't be scared of showing up somewhere with our hair in braids, afraid of something like this. We must realize how important it is for Native people (of all gender identities) to be able to choose for themselves how they wear their hair and express themselves in a settler colonial society.

When we moved to Atlanta in 2014, I began growing my hair out again. Our hair transforms with us throughout our lives, and while I have long hair today, I might cut if off again one day, because maybe I will be called to a different season of listening, of knowing, of asking. For now, a return to myself is a return to a tradition that has long held me.

Daniel Heath Justice writes in his book *Why Indigenous Literatures Matter*, "In a world that so often wants to see us only as historical artifacts, writing about the now is a powerful refusal to disappear into the symbolic frontier of the settler colonial imaginary."[2]

Indigenous women and our cultures are not stuck in a past identity that is incapable of evolving; we are alive and well today, working and creating in ways that are unique to each of us, sharing stories and experiences that only we can share. But when the world operates on toxic stereotypes, we are not seen or heard as we *are*.

Something as everyday as the way I wear my hair is an act of resistance and survival against toxic stereotypes that silence, because while my hair does not define me completely, it is connected to who I am as a Potawatomi woman, whether it's worn in a long braid or not. My hair has always been part of me, and it always will be. However I choose to wear it is sacred because it belongs to this life season, and it belongs to my growth as a woman and as an Indigenous person too. Seasons drive our world, just as they drove the world of my ancestors, and taught them how to live, how to adapt and survive through studying the medicines of the earth, through remembering who came before and dreaming of who comes next. My hair moves with me through these seasons, as something I can shift and change, something that follows me in my experiences and reminds me that something new is always beginning.

❦

During Black History Month 2019, Virginia governor Ralph Northam was criticized for a picture in his high school yearbook in which he participated in the racist act of wearing blackface. Over the next few weeks, a series of conversations began on social media, sparking discussions of real issues about our education system, about what is and isn't racism in our schools. For Native peoples, these incidents also sparked conversations about the problems we face in public schools, from racist mascots named after toxic stereotypes of Indigenous peoples to the fact that for many students the only time they hear about Natives is during Thanksgiving, when children as young as preschool age are taught to make cheap headdresses out of paper and glue. An article released in February of that year talked about the blackface-versus-redface conversation, stating, "Blackface and redface are not the same, but they are fruit of the same poisonous tree—namely, white supremacy."[3] This is an important conversation to be had in America, a conversation that stems from the very foundations of white supremacy, which produced a culture of toxic whiteness in 2019 and continues that toxicity today. Unveiling how we prepare our children to be adults through school systems can be terrifying on many levels, but the trauma inflicted on Native parents every year when Thanksgiving and Columbus Day roll around is exhausting to say the least.

I struggled with what to tell my son's kind teacher when I knew he was receiving confusing messages about his own identity and how it fits in a history book. I struggled with how to tell the school that they were teaching my children that, in essence, their own Native kin must have died a long time ago. What confusion must this cause for my five-year-old, a boy who ends up separating his own Potawatomi identity from the Natives talked about in history books, those who, they say, *befriended Pilgrims and then happened to get sick at some point and die.* Everything we teach our children becomes part of them, and we cannot deny that. If Indigenous children see cartoons of Indians shooting bows and arrows at cowboys and unsuspecting pioneers, they will begin to imagine their own relatives as those *merciless savages,* exactly what we've been called throughout history. We must hold our education system accountable for the racist attitudes it instills and allows, and we must speak up when the truth isn't told. Children do not learn the glorious diversity of Indigenous peoples in the US, throughout North America, or even throughout the world. They learn the version of us told through a white man's eyes, a version portrayed in an old western or in Disney's *Peter Pan* and *Pocahontas.* I had a Pocahontas Barbie doll growing up, one just like the character in the Disney movie. But she was a *character,* one that does not tell anything close to the real and tragic story of Matoaka, who was kidnapped and brutally abused by English colonists. When I looked at that doll as a young girl, I saw myself. In the confusion of identity, I saw a Native woman with long black hair and dark skin, a Native woman who could sing to the wind and get a response. I grew up with a myth, and as an adult, I have to separate out what is true and what isn't. I have to ask myself what myths were embedded so deeply in me that they actually caused me to look at myself differently, to tell myself the story that whiteness tells. Our education system should work to tell the truth about racism, to tell the truth about why blackface is wrong and why Indigenous peoples often suffer silently.

It will take the work of parents, teachers, and administrators—everyone—working together in community to make sure this happens. Right after Thanksgiving, I went to both my children's classrooms to read a book to the kids, and I chose *The Mishomis Book* by Ojibwe author Edward Benton-Banai. I took that book so that those children would know *we are still here, and we still have languages and stories.* I told them that there are 573 federally recognized nations in the US, and many more that aren't recognized.[4] I told them that we have our own languages and stories, and I watched as my boys swelled with pride that *they are Potawatomi.* I taught the kids the Ojibwe word for *wolf,* ma-en'-gun, and they howled every time I read it. I watched as they tried to connect the dots in their little heads between what I was saying in real time and what they heard in the Thanksgiving narrative.

What if our children didn't have to be confused about that narrative? What if they were to hear exactly what is true and grow up with the power to change history because they know from the beginning that things are not as they should be and that Indigenous peoples should be treated with respect? Maybe then we wouldn't have people taking DNA tests to "prove" something that cannot be proven with race science. Maybe then Indigenous peoples wouldn't have to tweet about how inappropriate and problematic Indian mascots are. Maybe then Indigenous students could wear their regalia on their graduation robes and hats without being punished for it. Maybe then we wouldn't have to fight about the tomahawk chop or explain to young women why a "Pocahottie" Halloween costume is racist and upholds toxic patriarchy.

Maybe then we might be seen and valued for who we are today and who we have always been.

7

A Heart Language

WHEN I WAS IN GRADE SCHOOL, I checked out a book on the Scottish Gaelic language from the local library. On long drives, I would sit in the back seat of the car learning a new language as best I could. With every phrase, I was catching a new piece of a mystery, like solving a puzzle of a picture I had never seen. Language can do that to us because it connects us to each other, somehow revealing both an individual cultural characteristic and the oneness of humanity, all at once.

Language is the thin thread that holds cultures together, and when it is threatened, we lose so much. I don't remember any of the phrases I learned in that book, but I remember how it felt, sitting in the back seat of the car, unlocking a secret, learning of a people who lived and breathed for centuries before me.

In the late 1800s, the US government opened its first Indian boarding school, led by army officer Richard Pratt. "A great general has said that the only good Indian is a dead one," Pratt said. "In a sense, I agree with the sentiment, but only in this: that all the Indian there is in the race should be dead. Kill the Indian in him, and save the man."[1]

Hundreds of other schools opened after Carlisle, all created to assimilate Indigenous children so that, eventually, Indigenous culture would cease to exist. The government and the church came alongside each other to make the children in the schools both more Westernized and more "Christian," because America itself was built on the premise of a colonizing Christian empire. One of the most essential ways to "kill the Indian" was to strip children of their language, thus destroying a lifeline to their culture. School teachers cut the children's hair, burned their clothes, and destroyed any remnants of their home that they may have brought along with them. In the days, months, and years following, teachers indoctrinated the children with white culture, with ideas of Christian salvation, and with the most important white supremacist idea of all: that who they were and where they came from was an abomination that must be put to death for good. If children were caught speaking their language, they were punished, and the rates of sexual and physical abuse were horrifyingly high. These boarding schools were filled with abuse and neglect of all kinds, stories that we'd never openly talk about in church or even in American society at large.

Ongoing trauma was evident in the way entire generations of Indigenous peoples left those boarding schools (if they didn't die while they were there) unable to reconnect to their cultures, often stripped of memories and the ability to understand who they were and where they came from. We are seeing this mirrored today in our immigration policies under the Trump administration, as families seeking asylum at the border and people who have lived in the US for years are suddenly being torn away from one another, and as children are put in cages in detention centers where they are abused, neglected, and in some cases killed. Because we do not value immigrants' lives, we do not value immigrant families or Indigenous immigrant cultures. It is ironic: a government that won't welcome people who aren't *American enough* is the same government that was once full of outsiders, a government that came from a group who forced their way onto a land already inhabited, took over, and eventually became the ones forcing others to assimilate.

Many of our ancestors were unable to communicate much of the trauma they faced in boarding schools and were instead forced to sit in shame and silence over things they could not control. Later generations of Indigenous children weren't taught the language, and it seemed that boarding schools did exactly what they set out to do—to strip us of our identity. Many of us grew up with grandparents who did not speak a word about our identities. Boarding schools were only part of the wound. Native children were also taken from their families and adopted into white families in order to continue that erasure, and Indigenous communities are still fighting these battles today. But despite the efforts to erase us, our languages are alive, and many of us are beginning to learn them, to practice them, to listen to them wherever and however we can, because we know what it means to lose something that sits at the very heart of our cultures. Indigenous peoples who did not grow up with their people are reconnecting and returning so that they can know who they are. Language revitalization projects are happening all over this land, and non-Native people should celebrate this work. In the Potawatomi tribe, only ten fluent language teachers remain, and it is important that for future generations, we are remembering why it matters that we learn our language, that we know ourselves, so that who we are is not further erased.

I did not grow up learning to speak Potawatomi or knowing that the language itself even existed. The only language I learned growing up was English, except for the Spanish I studied in high school or the Russian I studied in college. I had no idea that we as Potawatomi people had our own language, a language that connects us back to our identity, that allows us to know our stories and our unique way of experiencing the world. I listened to the Potawatomi language for the first time over my laptop speakers while I made dinner one afternoon a few years ago. I heard the speaker from Citizen Potawatomi Nation tell me words I had never memorized, hardly heard, that still speak to me in ways that move every fiber of my being. I stood there with tears in my eyes, because the things I did not yet understand were the things I seemed to so desperately need: to speak the language spoken by my ancestors, years ago, before we were forced out of our home, before we were assimilated into a white culture that wanted only English spoken. The first thing I memorized was a Potawatomi prayer, one that I use often instead of praying in English. It gives me a different space with Creator, *Mamogosnan*, Great Mystery, *Kche Mnedo* than I've had before, a space that I cannot reach in any white American church. Potawatomi author Robin Wall Kimmerer says, "Our language sounds like wind in the pines and water over rocks, sounds our ears may have been more delicately attuned to in the past, but no longer. To learn again, you really have to listen."[2]

Our language teaches us to tune our souls back to the land, *Segmekwe*, who has always held us. Our language reminds us that we come from dust and we will return to that dust, our souls floating and resting in the magic of the galaxies and the cosmos. I began an online course to learn the Potawatomi language, to have something to pass down to my children and to their children after them. I sat at my white desk by the window in my bedroom while my three-year-old napped on the bed, and I took notes and quizzes and breathed in and out the old and sacred words.

Language is wrapped around everything else in a culture, no matter what you speak or where you're from. It's sacred, connected to identity, to ethnicity, to soul, to Mystery. It is the way we move, the way our hearts speak, the lens through which we see the world. Without language, we are lost. I know that this language-learning will be our legacy, the thin line that carries us generations down the road. It will take time, and it constantly feels like I'm taking ten steps back and one step forward, but every step forward is grounding me in who I am and have always been.

As a child, without knowing my own Potawatomi language, I may have missed understandings of God other than what I received within the traditional Southern Baptist churches I was part of. Knowing, for example, why we go to powwows, the significance of ceremony, dancing as prayer, the important rhythm of the drums, and the connectedness of community might have given me a different idea of how we build community in a lasting and sustainable way. I might have understood why the trees have so much to teach us and why water should be protected. That is why it matters so much that many Native people are returning, despite the work of the church and the American government to break those ties. The day I learned what the word *America* meant in Potawatomi, I was reminded again of what we've lost and of the importance of returning again to our own words. Potawatomi is not English; our Potawatomi words have so much meaning behind them. The word for America, *kchemokmanke*, translates loosely to "white person with long knives," referring to the Europeans who invaded our lands and butchered our people. This is why language matters: it helps us understand where we come from and what it means to be Indigenous. Our language carries our stories and experiences, and for as long as whiteness has tried to steal that, we have continued to be who we have always been, and we will pass that on to our children.

⚬—❀—⚬

Languages carry stories. Oral Indigenous societies pass family and cultural stories down generation to generation to preserve culture. To be able to hear one of our Potawatomi stories in Potawatomi is an absolute honor, because it connects me back to who we once were and who we still are today. Even though colonization has taken so much from us, telling our creation narrative or our winter stories, even in English, still means something. Telling our experiences, like I'm expressing my experiences to you in this book, is a sacred kind of work, and as we pass our stories and experiences down to our children, we are changing our children, changing ourselves, and changing the world.

In 2017 I hosted an event in our city focused on the conversation surrounding Indigenous people and the events that unfolded in Standing Rock, North Dakota. The Dakota Access Pipeline was originally set to go through Bismarck, North Dakota, a predominantly white city, but it was rerouted to go through an area near the Standing Rock Sioux reservation, so that it impacted Indigenous peoples and their water supply. In response, Indigenous peoples and their allies gathered from all over the world to fight against a pipeline that would poison the water in Lake Oahe and the Missouri River. The event was created to give voice to Indigenous peoples and allies who went to Standing Rock to show support to water protectors, and as someone who did not go to Standing Rock, I wanted to listen, engage, and learn for myself. As the event drew closer, many of the people who were going to share were unable to come, so there were only a few of us left. I decided to open up the microphone to anyone attending and make it a public storytelling event. My friend Jonathan from the Navajo Nation stepped up to the microphone. He reminded us that we belong to each other, that we must stick together and have honest conversations for the sake of a better future. I deeply felt every word, remembering how much language and expression matter, how important it is that we speak to each other in peace and with honesty, especially when we are so divided around so many things. Can you imagine if all over the country we hosted storytelling events, inviting people to step up to a microphone? Yes, it could go wrong, but it could also go so right when people are given space to lead with vulnerability and humility. People could tell their stories of surviving trauma, their stories of beating cancer or still fighting against it. Others might tell about what it's like to be a queer woman of color in America or a Sikh man in America who battles hate crimes against his community daily. Still others might talk about what it's like to be lonely or in love or both. You see, our human expressions, no matter how varied, still bring us together in ways that we cannot always understand, and language is the force that guides us.

One of the church's biggest blind spots is ignoring the stories of those on the outside. We hide behind dogma and theology instead of leaning into our humanity to connect with one another or to the land. But when we stop to look out a window and see what is happening outside, or when we step outside the door of our home to breathe the fresh, cold air, we are taking in the stories of the earth. As Anishinaabe author Richard Wagamese writes, "When you break the connection that binds you to money, time, obligations, expectations and concerns, the land enters you. It transports you."[3] And when we step back into those spaces again, those spaces filled with noise, we have stories to tell. I find that when I go outside to listen to the language that only the land speaks, she sends me back with poetry. She sends me back with a connectedness to both her soul and mine that can be expressed only in words that have rhythm and movement and life to them.

> When the wind blows, we imagine she is erasing every
> injustice,
> sweeping misdoings from the east to the west,
> making room for something new, a more whole world.
> Instead, what we don't realize is that she is rustling the
> tree branches
> to sing us a song.
> Instead, she is sowing seeds across the landscapes,
> seeds that tomorrow will become the beauty that
> restores us.
> Instead, she is whispering for us to hold on, to keep
> going,
> to water those seeds, because one day, they will show us
> the way home.

Poetry is life to us and to those around us. Throughout time, our poets are often our prophets, the ones who dance and sing and write, expressing things we did not know were stirring inside us for years. Our poets, our storytellers, are the bridge between the languages of the earth and our spoken languages, between the stories of the earth and our stories. May we all learn what it means to be poets who step outside and back inside, made new, sacred language flowing from our lips to and for one another.

—⬣—

We live in an era in which we are beginning to dig deeper into questions of how we got here. We are asking why there is so much injustice, why so many of our police are corrupt, why Black men can't kneel during the national anthem, and why a holiday called Columbus Day is offensive. Language creates cultures, cultures create nations, and leaders of nations tend to write history, and we must ask what our language evokes, whether we are using it for good or for evil.

We live in a time when Black people, Indigenous people, and other people of color are speaking up, sharing our stories, redefining what it means to be alive in America—but let's acknowledge that many of these people have been speaking up for a long time and are only now being heard, if heard at all.

Thanksgiving 2018 was a really difficult time for me. Native American Heritage Month happens in November, so while we are celebrating that we are still here, we are bombarded with Thanksgiving myths and people asking us for all the resources they should have been asking about any other month of the year. Kind, well-intentioned parents message me asking for book lists to read to their children, churches email me asking for Thanksgiving reflections that don't center celebration of Pilgrims or sometimes even inviting me to preach, unpaid, on a topic that is really difficult for me, and I struggle to find the right language to express my exhaustion.

In 2018, when my inboxes were full of these messages, I finally went to my social media accounts and made an announcement asking people to stop messaging me, to do the work themselves, and to stop expecting Indigenous peoples to give more than we already give every day of the year, especially at Thanksgiving. It is a time of confusion and mourning, and I honestly don't have anything left to give others in that space. Non-Native people responded, held me up, thanked me for speaking, and some of my white friends apologized. One friend sent me a gift a few months later, with a note of both thanks and apology, a bag of coffee mailed with it. I drank that coffee and thought of my friend every day, thought of the kind of ally she wants to become. We all make mistakes in these conversations, and we have to be willing to step beyond our fear of saying the wrong thing to ask hard questions and have honest conversations about where we go from here. My non-Native friends have to understand that the myths told at Thanksgiving only continue the toxic stereotypes and hateful language that has always been spewed at us, and they have to do the work to educate themselves about a better way. Roxanne Dunbar-Ortiz and Dina Gilio-Whitaker wrote a book on this topic called *"All the Real Indians Died Off": And 20 Other Myths about Native Americans*. In the introduction, they write, "For five centuries Indians have been disappearing in the collective imagination. They are disappearing in plain sight."[4]

Indigenous peoples cannot fight against these mistruths alone. Conversations about replacing Columbus Day with Indigenous Peoples Day shouldn't be happening just once every year or just within circles of Native people. It should be discussed in city planning meetings, and our street signs should be renamed if they carry traumatic names or celebrate the people who committed atrocities throughout history, because language is about the fabric of a place, what we create, how we explain who we are, who God is, and what the responsibility of those in power must be. To be a place of "we the people," we have to be a place that is truly *for all people,* and how do we do this if we don't talk about the stolen land that America rests on? How do we do this if we don't talk about Confederate monuments and schools named after racists? The answer is with all of us; to tell the truth is to give language to experiences that are often ignored by society.

8

Gifts of Prayer

To be truly wise is to understand that knowing and not knowing are one. Each has the power to transform.

Richard Wagamese, *One Story, One Song*

THE GIFTS OF PRAYER—of sweetgrass, sage, tobacco, and cedar—are said to have been given to us to keep us connected to *Segmekwe*, Mother Earth, to share her good gifts and to ask Creator to hear us, to be present with us. As a Potawatomi person, I pray to remember, and I pray to keep the *shkodé*, the fire, lit inside of me. One story says that Creator gifted *sema*, or tobacco, to the Potawatomi people, but they did not know at first how to use it. They had to learn how to use it, how to honor it, and how to teach the people to honor it. This plant was given to us so that when we grow it, dry it, and lay it down in a sacred place or smoke it in our pipes, we remember who we are and that we belong to the earth.

These ceremonies teach Potawatomi people what it means to slow down and pray, to remember who we are and what it means to be cleansed. The day our boys started public school, we prayed together in Potawatomi and smudged, taking our sage and wafting the smoke over our heads to remember that *Mamogosnan* is with us. We talked about what it means to remember who we are, to know who our ancestors are. My oldest son began his prayer in Potawatomi, and I was overcome with emotion, because I knew that he will understand something I didn't as a child, that our Potawatomi sense of knowing and being is taking root inside him every day, and nothing can erase that, despite the fact that when we pray, we remember that we have been kept from praying.

Laws in the US have been created to keep Indigenous people from practicing religious ceremony for generations, whether it's the Sun Dance or simply burning sage for morning prayers in school; it wasn't until 1978 that the American Indian Religious Freedom Act was passed. Still, our religious and spiritual expressions and ceremonies are often criticized. Even in 2019, high school students were targeted for wearing feathers on their graduation caps and punished for wearing regalia, and others fight for their children to keep their hair in braids or to smudge as an act of cultural and religious expression. Things that are so essential to many Indigenous people as a way of life are seen as trivial, evil, or strange to the white world around us. The sacred sage that is a gift from the earth is packaged inside a "witch kit" at Sephora to draw in consumers. The life of prayer for Indigenous peoples is not something that should be stolen or appropriated.

Growing up in the Baptist tradition, I heard little mention of communicating with God through the earth. On Sundays, we would often hear sermons about how prayer is something we should just *try harder at*, instead of something we enter into. When I began to pray in Potawatomi, I understood something different about prayer—that it is a holistic act that involves all of me, and all of the creatures around me, communing with God.

If we truly believe that God surrounds us, we believe that prayer is an everyday experience of being alive. It may not look the same for me as it does for you; you won't practice the way

I practice as a Potawatomi woman, but when you step outside and engage with the world in quiet listening, prayer will happen, and it will take on its own way of being for you. Perhaps prayer is just poetry, and we are living the expressions of what it means to be human. This is why Creator gave us gifts to remember. This is why, when I burn sage or lay tobacco down, I know that I am tethered to a love that has remained steady throughout the centuries and that always calls me back to its own sacredness. And that sacredness will always lead me back out to the world to do the work of love.

Prayer is always an invitation.

—◆—

Georgia's popular Stone Mountain State Park is one of the first hiking spots our family discovered when we moved to Atlanta, when we wanted to get to know the land. Not long after we discovered it, we learned that the mountain face contains a famous carving of the Confederate generals known to the South. There is an intense juxtaposition: this land, now considered a celebration of the Confederacy, is also land with so much history, a place that sheltered both the Muscogee Creek and Cherokee peoples as well. How do we celebrate the land while we mourn what has been done to it?

Jemar Tisby says in his book *The Color of Compromise*, "All too often, Christians name a few individuals who stood against the racism of their day and claim them as heroes. They fail to recognize how rarely believers made public and persistent commitments to racial equality against the culture of their churches and denominations."[1] Because people gather at Stone Mountain State Park to hike, to rest on the water, to get to know the land of Georgia, without recognizing it as land that was once inhabited by the Muscogee Creek and Cherokee peoples (many who are still here), prayers over this land have become prayers of praise for the Confederacy. Prayers in this place have become prayers of white supremacy to a white supremacist god, the same god who drove out the Indigenous people and enslaved African people in this place. We have to ask ourselves why and how we pray, and what our prayers do in places that are called sacred but have been harmed. We have to ask what the prayers in our churches do, what they teach us about our own ways of seeing the world.

When I come to this park, I bring tobacco. I hear the trees speaking, and they remember everything. As the rocks invite me to sit, they're asking me to take a moment to remember. And when the water stills to reflect the blue Georgia sky, I am being asked to remember, to reclaim something. So I lay my tobacco on the water's surface and whisper, "You're not forgotten." I listen to the ancestors and to the created world that longs to tell its own stories. I whisper a prayer to *Kche Mnedo*, to *Mamogosnan*, Creator, who never forgets, who knows the language of every tribe and tongue. *New York Times* bestselling Cheyenne and Arapaho author Tommy Orange writes, "Being Indian has never been about returning to the land. The land is everywhere or nowhere."[2] If we listen, the land is speaking. If we listen, we are doing the active work of paying attention, not only to our own lives but also to history telling its own story again and again.

Sitting near the water, I hear people talking, their voices echoing through the trees, across the water from the other side of the hiking trail. They laugh, and I think of the people who once laughed there as they washed their bodies and clothes in that water. I see a kayaker and think of trading routes and the work of survival. The land in this place does not belong to me, and yet I allow my presence here to receive something, to consider what was lost and what can never be truly forgotten.

The water never stops mirroring. Rocks never stop being foundations. Trees never stop breathing, giving us breath to go on. And history never stops being true, if we can only look her in the eyes and ask for that truth. I wonder, How long has it been since someone laid tobacco on the water, asked the water to speak, fed her? We forget that we are not the only hungry ones who need to communicate our hunger. We restore and reclaim things from the grip of hate the best way we know how, not because it is ours to restore out of a sense of ownership, but because the work of love is never finished. One day, that carving on the side of the mountain will be gone, eroded away by the forces of Mother Earth herself, but the mountain itself will remain, our prayers and the prayers of the ancestors holding it up all the time.

I bought *Caleb's Crossing* by Geraldine Brooks a few years ago when we first moved to Atlanta, and it stayed tucked away, without thought, in my room in our apartment. It's a book about a young Puritan woman's relationship with a young man from the Wampanoag tribe, based on the true story of the first Native man to graduate from Harvard. I saw the book on the shelf one day and decided to pick it up and read it. The day before I finished reading it, I saw a sign outside an Episcopal church in our city with the name *Geraldine Brooks* across the front. I knew in that moment that I wanted to meet this Australian woman who had written a historical fiction book about the Wampanoag people and their erasure and assimilation into Western ideas and society.

As she signed my book after the event, I told Brooks that I was Potawatomi, that I was processing and embracing my identity as an Indigenous woman. I told her that her words helped me on the journey. She stopped writing, looked into my eyes where I was stooped down in front of the table, and smiled. "Your ancestors will be glad to have you back," she said.

Sometimes, we are brought back to ourselves in the least likely of ways. Sometimes, allies come alongside us to remind us who we are. Sometimes, sacred gifts of community become the gifts of prayer we need to get us through.

During a particularly difficult news cycle for Indigenous peoples, my friend Tuhina sent me a gift in the mail. Tuhina wrote in a card a truth that she herself knows well as a Brown-skinned woman living in Trump's America: "Multiple truths can exist in the same being at the same time," she wrote, and I thought to myself, *this is exactly what my life has always been.*

For so long, I was told to pray only the way the Baptists prayed, to see the world the way American Christians see the world. I was told that the white perspective is the only perspective, but now I have seen from the perspectives of so many. Prayer is a layered, complicated thing, and when we approach it that way, we enter into the mystery of what it is, of what it means to gather in community to choose sacredness around us. Duality, or living in a way that constantly propels us toward one extreme or the other, divides us by binary thinking and it steals our ability to enter into sacredness, making us into people who pray to get a reward, who pray because we are afraid we will be punished if we don't.

The problem with the dualities of our thinking—black versus white, good versus bad, light versus dark—is that they leave no room for those of us who wish to exist and explore outside those binaries and in those liminal spaces. It requires conversations laced with nuance. It reminds us that life is complicated and conversations about healing are necessary. The people I look to are the ones who pray the way their ancestors prayed and who remember that the world is not ruled by whiteness but by the diverse beauty of humanity and creation, the people who are constantly working to give thanks to a good, good world.

PART 2 SUMMARY

While each of us in the world searches for who we are, we are also searching for how we must respond to the things of the earth that we do not understand. Searching, digging deep, praying, looking for treasures, means that we cannot give up on humility, on childlikeness. Looking pain in the face, failing and trying again, these are the things that bring us back to sacred Mystery. Once we search, we find. Once we see, we cannot un-see. The search, therefore, leads us to the *truth*, no matter how beautiful or horrifying those truths may be. What we do with that truth is up to us.

PART 3

The Struggle
for Truth

Muskrat died while he dove into the water for a piece of the
   earth.
He sacrificed his life so that all creatures might know the land
   again.
He held the dirt in his paws and brought it to the surface of
   the water,
to his kin who waited anxiously for a sign,
to see if a new world might be possible.

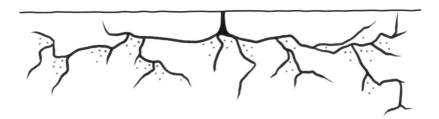

God is more language than this.
God is more breath than lungs,
more oxygen than air,
more wind than atmosphere
in which to hold it.

God is more soul than us.
God is more time than schedules,
more grace than boundaries,
more everything than the imaginable.

And yet, we are constricted.
And yet, we say
language must be spoken,
breath must be breathed,
oxygen must revive.

We say
wind is the only spirit,
this soul is the end of us,
time rules the world,
grace is unreachable,
and everything is bound,
linear, and fathomed.

What, then, is God?

God is
exactly everything that is
and everything that we do not know of—
Mystery stacked upon Mystery,
Sacred enveloping Sacred,
Treasure buried within the pebbles
of our earth-kingdoms.

9

Ceremony

I n 2019, the United Methodist Church met in a special session to discuss whether they would participate in or allow the ordination and marriage ceremonies of LGBTQ+ people in the church. They voted to maintain a "traditional plan" that denies the rights of LGBTQ+ people to serve freely in pastoral ministry, a decision that directly ostracizes many who have belonged to the denomination for decades. It is heartbreaking when the table of God is not set for all the people of God. It is heartbreaking when colonization and patriarchy take root over the truth, which manifests in inclusive love.

We live in an era in which pastors and other church leaders can almost immediately receive criticism for what they preach or say via social media outlets like Twitter. While this can be intimidating, and I can't imagine leading people in such a space, there are so many in this world who are asking to be heard, who have been ignored for far too long. If we cannot solve all the world's problems, we can at least make sure that as leaders we are actively speaking and working to dismantle systems that oppress. This means that the communion table in our churches is a political table. This means that the communion table is a table that speaks on social issues of oppression. This means that the communion table is a table set for those no one else wants to serve. The communion table is a table for all bodies and all souls and all people seeking to know what it might mean to feel the sacred pulse of Mystery around us and in us.

One quiet afternoon a few years ago, while everyone in my family was napping, I slipped out the front door to get a package my friend Shelley left for me. In a three-page letter, she outlined the reasons for giving me a handmade communion set she ordered from a Lakota artist. A few months earlier I had quit my job as a worship leader at a progressive church so that I would have more time to write and travel for speaking events, and also because I was feeling an increasing tension between my ability to be a leader in the church and to tell my own story as a Potawatomi woman. I have been a church leader in some capacity ever since I was about eleven years old. Whether I was singing in the choir or leading 6 a.m. Bible studies at a coffee shop in my small Missouri town, I took on responsibilities in the church. As I've grown older and started the work of deconstructing *and decolonizing*, I find that church leadership is more difficult, because I do not fit as easily into the mold made for me at a young age.

After moving to Georgia and serving at this church as the interim worship leader, I was suddenly struck with the reality that if I fight the effects of assimilation in my life, *if I speak from my Potawatomi self instead of the whiteness I've been trained and taught to live through*, the church will increasingly see me as a threat. They will get *uncomfortable*, and they will question my faith, because it doesn't look like the faith shaped by the forefathers of the church. In essence, the church wants what is white in me, but not what is Native in me. Committees met to discuss whether I was making the church look good as I wrote online pieces questioning the role of the church in oppressing

Indigenous peoples throughout history. Some church leaders encouraged me as a worship leader but discouraged my voice as an Indigenous woman seeking reconciliation between the church and injustices done toward marginalized communities. I chose to leave, realizing that even the progressive spaces that claim to want change don't necessarily want what that change requires—giving up white supremacy.

But that day, Shelley's letter was a gentle reminder that I am seen and known, and that *all of me* is the thing I must speak from. The deep blue designs etched onto white pottery are the only reminder I need, that somehow every part of who I am is called to that communion table and gives me the ability to call others to that table, no matter what tribe or tongue, no matter how broken or bruised. If we are to believe that the inclusive love of God is real, we'd better start building a bigger table. If we are truly to hold the space of *all tribes and tongues*—because the diversity of the world is included in the love of God—we'd better get to work breaking down systems of colonization wherever we find them. As a woman, Shelley knows what it is like to be told she can't be what she is called to be as a church leader because her gender won't allow it. But that communion table and those elements, they say otherwise.

The predominantly white, Western church has issues with what it means to truly practice community with *all* people, and that is seen in the problem of individualism in our churches, a problem that goes against the idea behind the communion table. While we sit in pews singing songs about personal sins and salvation, we are ill equipped to go into the world to face systems of injustice, many of which we helped create. We are ill prepared to actually engage the communal power of grace and love. James Cone, the founder of Black liberation theology, once said in an interview, "I read the Bible from the bottom."[1] If American Christians were truly to read the Bible from the bottom, we might look around to see who the poor, tired, and oppressed are, and if we truly saw, we'd get rid of our doors and our walls and our dogmas altogether, and we'd put those tables outside.

Genocide of Indigenous peoples, the slave trade, masters proclaiming salvific dominion over other human beings through the power of whiteness—these are all elements that have led us to a white supremacist and individualistic faith, and we are separated from truly practicing community, from understanding the truth of kinship. Our communion tables become, instead of body and blood, nationalism and homophobia or white supremacy and indifference. If we cannot go into our faith spaces proclaiming a narrative that is inclusive for *everyone*, how are we supposed to, throughout the week, proclaim a narrative of love that is for the poor, women, immigrant, tired, queer, or abused? If we stand on Sunday and sing songs about personal sins, how are we to go out and challenge institutional systems of *hate*? The answer is that our communion table, a gathering place of community, must really be a table of *communing*.

—⚘—

The first time I attended a powwow as an adult, I cried through the Grand Entry. Floods of memories came back to me from when I was young, from those times I attended powwows in Oklahoma, watching people dance and hearing drums keep the beat of the dance. Back then, I didn't understand what was happening. I had no context to know that the drum and the song and the dance go together as worship, as something beautifully sacred. So as an adult, every time I enter the powwow arena, I feel my feet become grounded. I feel everything slow down, from my pulse to the world around me. The first time I entered, it was with my oldest son, Eliot. We walked in together, holding hands, and he slowly began to separate himself from me, lost in dance, lost in community with the people around him. He followed closely behind two women, watching their jingle dresses sway as they moved. I watched in awe, understanding that to know who we are is to know what it means to embody these expressions of identity, to commune with the earth.

In some ways, the powwow scene has become a space where non-Natives can come and watch people perform in "costumes," where they can buy T-shirts with wolves on them and watch demonstrations about how Indians used to live in tipis. Despite the efforts of Indigenous peoples to share our cultures, encounters between Native and non-Native people often reinforce problematic stereotypes, and that can be difficult to see. So sometimes at the powwow, I make eye contact with the people who walk by me. I watch the dancers intently. I let the drum beat along with my heart and I remember why all of this matters to us as Indigenous peoples. Yet, throughout history our cultures have been demonized and our dance mocked. Native people deserve safe places to dance and to pray, to remember who we are and why ceremony matters.

It is not the job of the Indigenous peoples of America to educate non-Natives on what is or isn't appropriate, and yet we do it every day. We provide resources, we teach classes on how to break stereotypes, we tweet book lists and share the work of Native artists, activists, and academics who are working to re-shape and decolonize our systems of thought. This is holy and sacred work, yet it often comes at a cost. It is exhausting to relive our generational trauma, to tell the stories of history that are so often covered up and twisted by narratives of whiteness. We know about the communion tables in the church sanctuary, but what about the communion tables outside? What if communion is also found in the sacred places that have always held room for us: the trees that have always said, "Come, sit in my shade and rest," the water that says, "Come, bathe and drink and be refreshed," the grasses that say, "Come and dance with me," and the seasons that say, "Come, learn what it means to live a whole life"? This is what I hear when I go outside. This is what my ancestors experienced when they communed by the maple trees and tended to the wild rice stalks rising out of the water.

If you're on social media long enough, you'll see memes during the holidays about difficult family conversations around the dinner table. Families that are split politically, socially, even theologically come together to ask what it means to be family in all its complexities.

For our family of six (dogs included), we are asking what the holidays will look like as our children grow older, as we examine what it means to be a family of both Potawatomi and European people. We are asking how to honor my partner's German and French heritage as well as the people I descend from. It's a conversation many mixed families have throughout the year.

A few years ago I began serving Indigenous dishes for the holidays, incorporating our Potawatomi stories into our holiday experiences. When we gather for meals, we are eating wild rice, ordered from Winona LaDuke's Honor the Earth organization in Minnesota. We are remembering and telling stories that often go untold in most American households. Instead of honoring a myth about Pilgrims and Indians gathered at a table, can we choose to honor the resilience of Indigenous peoples who are still alive today, reviving our own traditions that teach us to see the earth as good and sacred?

For Christmas a few years ago, I made a Potawatomi wild rice dish with fresh berries and maple syrup, a recipe from Mariah Gladstone, who runs Indigikitchen, an online resource of cooking videos for Indigenous dishes. Mariah is not only helping non-Natives know that our cultures are alive through our food; she is also helping people like me reconnect with our sacred foods. When I made Potawatomi wild rice and berries for Christmas at my in-laws' house that year, I told everyone about the wild rice, and as we sat around the table eating, I knew we would not be forgotten. As long as we make these foods that keep us tethered to who we are and to the land, our holidays will mean something other than the myths we tell in America to make white people feel good about history.

Chef Sean Sherman's book *The Sioux Chef's Indigenous Kitchen* is giving Indigenous people the courage to remember why our food is so important, why it is connected to ceremony, and why it is, in and of itself, sovereign and worthy of respect. The table is a sacred space, and Sean knows that. The cookbook is full not only of recipes but also of cultural stories, of the *reasons* why we eat the way we eat and what our traditions say about our food. I display the book in my kitchen, and I hope to slowly begin using the recipes in our everyday meals and also to simply educate the people who enter our home.

The tables in our homes are spaces that should be inclusive and welcoming, not only to people who think like we do but also to those who don't, to those who are journeying and searching for sacredness in their own lives. Just like the communion table of the church should meet both inside and outside the church's doors, so our own tables should be set to welcome a stranger and to go outside to meet strangers in our midst. Decolonizing our table means recognizing that sacredness moves and breathes all over the place, in all people, in all creatures, in all things, so communion becomes the space in which we say *everyone and everything is loved.*

The table of the holidays, the table that brings pain and cele-bration to it, resilience and mourning, is a table that allows us to know that history matters and that our conversations about it matter. If a cookbook sitting on my kitchen counter can re-mind someone that our food from the earth is sacred, *that is communion.* And if a wild rice dish I bring to the holiday table reminds someone of the earth's provision, we are returning. *We are returning back to the goodness of the earth, to her gifts, to our childlikeness, as ceremony leads us all the way home.*

10

Ancestors

MY FRIEND AMY PAULSON and I met at a park outside of Atlanta one summer day so that she could take headshots for my upcoming book. I met Amy through a mutual friend, and right away we clicked. Amy is a storyteller as much as she is a photographer, and as she took photos of me that day, she asked questions. She pulled emotions out of me, stories out of me, so that as I spoke, she captured each moment and each emotion in a photo.

At one point Amy asked a question about my children and my children's children, about what they might see when they look on my face, about how *proud they are to call me their kin.*

I realized then that one day I am going to be an ancestor. When I have passed on and my spirit is left to lead my children and their children, they will talk about me, about my legacy, about what I left undone or what I did to change things. I realized that these photos are an actual embodiment of sacred life, not just a headshot for a book. So, I remember my ancestors. I remember what they have left for me, and I remember what was left undone. I look at their pictures, searching their eyes for stories they may never have told us when they were alive. Instead, they visit us in dreams, reconnecting us, helping us imagine a new way forward, a way of peace. One day we will become ancestors, but until then, we whisper to our long-gone ones, asking that they remember us.

Passed On One,
I see you there.
Not your skin and bones,
nor the frame that once held you.
I see your aura,
your spirit,
your essence.

I see the glow of who you once were
and who you are today.
I see, somehow,
the imprint of what you've left me here.

It's not a thumbprint, but some other form
of spirit-code.
Somehow, the shape of you
carves lines into the essence of who I am.
Somehow, I am enough
because you were
enough.

Ancestor, your name will always be
the sound of breath in my lungs.

Ancestor, your face will always look
like the face of my own children.

Ancestor, your essence
will always feel like
the wind
when it slips

through the tree branches,
singing a song.

You, Dear One, lead me, still.

I feel the gifts you've left me
and I wonder how much more
is waiting.

I learn my own way as I
reckon with your mistakes
and realize that you were human once,
like I am human now.

I wonder how much you notice
from the other side.

What does God feel like?

I'll wait,
and one day,
you'll show me.

We shop at an international farmers market in our city, and on the weekends and around holidays, it is terribly crowded. We swerve in and out of the aisles alongside others who don't speak the same language as we do, and it's a picture of the rich diversity of the world in one small building. One weekend while shopping, we headed toward the sugar snap peas, then to the snap beans in the next bin. I stood beside two older women who were sorting through the little green poles, sifting the bad ones from the good ones, talking together as they worked. Suddenly, memories came rushing back to me, snapping the ends off beans with my Grandmother Pauline, washing blackberries in my Grandma Avis's sink, fresh from the prickly bushes outside.

I remembered smelling bacon and biscuits from Grandma Avis's kitchen. The matriarchs of both sides of my family were the sort of women who brought you into their everyday spaces with kindness and grace. They spoke like people who have seen things, who have lived difficult lives and have survived. We remember that their stories live on in our own years after they've passed on, and they visit us when we need it most.

My Potawatomi ancestors remind me of who I am in dreams and in the faces of my children, just as your ancestors remind you of the things you've seen and what future generations will hold. We learn how to do things and how not to do them from the people of the past, asking questions and carrying honesty on our lips. How else will our children know the way forward if they do not understand how they got here?

To be people who fight against systems of oppression, we must remember where we come from the best way we know how, and we must honor those stories. If they are stories in which we ourselves are born from a line of oppressors, we must make amends, and we must be honest about what that requires of us today. We must dedicate ourselves to the work of dismantling toxic systems, no matter which side of those systems we are on.

I've had conversations with dear friends here in the South who are struggling with the reality that they are descendants of slave owners. What does that mean for my friends today? What responsibility do they carry to have hard and necessary conversations, especially within their families and faith communities?

I think of my friend Rob Lee (a descendent of Robert E. Lee), who left his church when he was chastised for speaking out about the racism and discrimination Black people face in America. In choosing to leave that church and make his life about reparations and honest conversations, Rob speaks into spaces alongside his Black friends, asking for forgiveness for the sins of his ancestors. He is leaning into hard and beautiful work, the kind of work we are all called to do if we want to create an America that truly welcomes the outsider and remembers that it was built on the backs of the oppressed. Our ancestors remind us that we have a responsibility to one another today.

What does reconciliation look like and feel like? How is it possible that the descendants of the oppressed and the oppressor can come together over a cup of coffee and change the world?

"Talk of reconciliation alone, especially when it sounds like a call to forget the past and move on, threatens not only the future of particular communities but individual identities as well," write authors Emmanuel Katongole and Chris Rice in their book, *Reconciling All Things*.[1]

We must remember that the work we do today, the work of both honoring our ancestors and asking questions about what work they left for us, means we acknowledge that this is ultimately part of creating a better world. This means there is always work to do. This means that as we shape the future, we remember the past, because our ancestors lived it and shaped it, just as we live and shape our world today.

❖

On a two-day road trip with my family a few years ago, we realized halfway through the drive that we'd pass through Shawnee, Oklahoma, near the land where I was born, the land that brought me up in my early years. As the sign for Shawnee crept up right along our path, I realized we were only a few short miles away from our tribal headquarters.

This time I wasn't the child going with my father but the adult bringing my own two children into that space. We walked around the gift shop, where I looked at handmade necklaces, a basket full of braided sweetgrass, and Citizen Potawatomi Nation coffee mugs. I watched as my youngest son, Isaiah, stared at knives protected by glass doors and as my oldest, Eliot, looked at necklaces with bright pink and purple beads on them. We walked through the museum, looking at pictures and models of the way things used to be, gateways to stories told again and again by our people but not lived for a long time in our modern homes and lifestyles. We were communing with our ancestors there, letting their ways speak over us. We saw the way things are today, the way our tribe is working to remember, to return to ourselves and to our ways of knowing and understanding Mystery. Jewish mystic Abraham Joshua Heschel once said, "As a tree torn from the soil, as a river separated from its source, the human soul wanes when detached from what is greater than itself."[2] For just a little while, we were home in a way that is difficult to describe. For about a decade after my father left, due to the effects of assimilation and colonization, I was living a detached life, a life separated from the reality of my own identity. I was missing this essential way of knowing God—the *Potawatomi* way of knowing—and returning to Oklahoma on this trip reminded me that the tether of *Kche Mnedo* stretches to meet us, often when we don't even realize it.

When we got back in the car to leave Oklahoma, I mourned. I mourned a childhood that I still don't quite understand, and I mourned that I couldn't stay there longer to ask all the questions I had inside that had been waiting so long for answers. But I also left grateful, expectant for what the land might hold for me in the future, always an invitation.

In the summer of 2018, I went back to Oklahoma again with my children and partner to attend our tribe's summer reunion celebration. It was the first time I had ever attended, and I was nervous. I was expectant.

After a long road trip, we finally arrived. At the registration table, I pulled out my tribal ID and proudly handed it to the woman sitting in front of me. She gave us our name badges and we headed to the gathering, where people were playing traditional hand games and resting from the hot sun.

In my early childhood, I knew the poverty that many Potawatomi people in Oklahoma still struggle with. My parents struggled to make ends meet. We ate commodity foods supplied by the government to rural Oklahoma. We were treated at Indian clinics.

Stepping back onto the soil of Oklahoma after years of being away from it was like a time warp. It was my childhood before age nine, before my father left. It was a foundation that I'm still trying to understand, roots that still reach into that red soil. But our ancestors speak to us, not just when we are children but also as adults. They come to us in dreams and memories, reminding us who we are and where we come from. My ancestors speak to me from the red dirt of Oklahoma. They speak to me at the Great Lakes. They remind me that there are memories embedded deeply inside me that I must reach for, and that those memories may find me only through speaking the Potawatomi language, hearing our stories, or returning to the land.

You see, when you are working hard to simply survive, it's difficult to have room for anything else. It's difficult to wonder if you're doing things right when suicide rates of young people in the tribe are so high because the effects of intergenerational trauma and assimilation are ongoing. If children are too hungry to learn, how will they know who they are? Our tribe is working to revive the language. Young people are stepping up to teach classes on traditional arts, and the elders are passing their knowledge down to those who will come after. And so we remember our ancestors and the way they lead us. We remember everything they lost in the Trail of Death when they were forcefully removed to Kansas and later came to Oklahoma. We remember what assimilation and settler colonialism do to people, and we actively live into our present reality for the good of our people.

That trip to Oklahoma was everything it needed to be. It was a reminder that the Trail of Death brought us to this place and that the US government made promises it did not keep. It was a reminder that for my children to know who they are, they have a foundation on that same Oklahoma dirt and in the Great Lakes where they will journey with me, and that beyond it, a whole world of learning still waits for us in the spaces where our ancestors are singing songs of resilience.

11

Self, Examined

THE JOURNEY OF ADULTHOOD requires so much looking back, whether we like to admit it or not. It's strange to look back over our childhood memories with a new lens. It's strange to remember things we didn't think we'd stored deep inside ourselves.

Living in New Mexico as a child brought memories I will never let go of, memories that will not let go of me. I recognize that hope in the land, in the dirt where I played, the Russian olive trees that would drop their fuzzy fruit on the ground. I'd roll them in my fingertips, marveling at their soft presence.

One fall while in New Mexico, my family met up with my father, who I hadn't seen in a few years, at a coffee shop in Taos. We didn't talk much that day. My father has always been pretty easygoing and not much of a talker. He just hovers in a room, giving space in case someone needs it. His presence doesn't demand much from others, and I've always appreciated that about him. The trauma passed from one generation to the next in Indigenous communities cannot be ignored; I carry trauma that my father and his mother carried, whether we know how to express it or not. It should not surprise us that trauma is carried in our bodies because systems of oppression after oppression are stacked against us. The effects of oppression are many, one being increased health risks that cause Native people to die at higher rates than any other group in the US. For example, diabetes rates among Native people are 189 percent higher and suicide rates are 62 percent higher.[1]

We don't talk about our trauma, so my father and I were content to watch my boys in silence, every now and then accented by a chuckle from the both of us. My partner, Travis, sat quietly, engaging with grace. My half-brother was there too, a Malaysian-Potawatomi young man who I'd spent time rocking to sleep as a baby, singing to him in the early morning hours when I stayed with my dad and stepmom on weekends. He's looking ahead to college in a few years. He's growing up under the roof of my father, a roof that I didn't always have.

That afternoon, I didn't need much from my father. I was no longer the child who wanted desperately to be seen and known by him. I was no longer the mother who wanted to process parenthood. I didn't need to know right then from my father what it's like to be a Potawatomi man in America.

I just wanted to sit in silence with him. I just wanted the presence, because the truth is, I'd forgiven him for leaving a long time ago. The difficulty is sitting in the spaces after forgiveness, into which forgiveness itself leads us, because we do not often know what it looks like. It is a space in which love somehow both fills and lightens when it's with us.

After an hour and a half, we parted ways. No words could have filled the space better, the space between us that was asking both of us to be made whole—together.

The journey toward wholeness takes the brokenness of a Potawatomi father and his youngest daughter, puts them in a space together, and tells them to simply *be*.

The journey of knowing ourselves and examining who we are becoming always, somehow, begins with our parents, with the love we did or did not receive. Perhaps that's why we long for intergenerational relationships wherever we go, and perhaps that's why searching for truth always involves searching for community as well. When our journeys call us back to something, back to our own beginnings, the search for truth teaches us to ask what those stories mean to us. What does our body tell us about who we once were, who we are today, and who we'll be tomorrow? The journey of knowing where we began is always to journey toward who we want to be, no matter what truths we find in the search.

◦—❀—◦

One weekend a few years ago, I attended a spiritual retreat on Pueblo land in the desert, a gathering of activists, entrepreneurs, writers, artists, preachers, and leaders sitting under the teaching of Richard Rohr. A few years before, I took an introductory course on Franciscan theology taught by Rohr through the Center for Action and Contemplation. The course used language I could understand to ground me in my identity both as an Indigenous woman and as a Christian. After struggling to understand both my cultural identity and my religious one, this course helped me find a way forward, even as I knew I would continue to struggle. While on Pueblo land that weekend, I spent time remembering that the land is forever sacred, and that was all I needed. This course also challenged me to ask who I was becoming, and as I listened to the land, land that is often ignored, mistreated, and forgotten, I found myself angry and overwhelmed, not just with myself but with the systems of humanity that we have created to destroy the land. I realized that to know myself, I must come to terms with the treatment of the earth that I have been complicit in, and I must work to change things.

No matter what kind of work we do in the world, whether we are community organizers and activists or stay-at-home parents, we have work to do, and we can take part in caring for the earth and engaging in difficult and honest conversations. Often, our religious spaces are kept clean from these conversations, simply because the conversations don't seem important enough, or they seem too political. So we must remind ourselves that even the inner work we do to learn about ourselves and to reorient our souls toward caring for the earth is inherently political work, work that stretches into our families, our social circles, our communities, and our governments. We must ask ourselves what we value and hold sacred, and work from there.

Work in spiritual spaces with mystics can be particularly dangerous and difficult, especially when a "mystic" experience comes at the cost of someone's cultural identity. Often, spiritual retreats appropriate and erase the cultures they are trying to enlighten themselves with, and we must do more honest work when it comes to these spaces. During the retreat that weekend, I struggled with how I fit as a participant, but at the same time I knew that the Indigenous experience is important to conversations around activism and spirituality, and I'm willing to step into these spaces.

As we drove back to Georgia from New Mexico the day after the retreat, I cried, stopping to touch and thank the rocks, the sky, and the land as I departed. I cried as the landscape turned from New Mexico to Colorado, as the mountains grew higher and higher and we began to see aspen trees on either side of the highway. I cried for Indigenous voices that will never be heard, and I cried in gratitude for the space in which my voice *was heard*. I cried because I had somehow returned home and yet was going back home at the same time.

━─❀─━

In America, we are obsessed with unrealistic and sometimes dangerous diets and resolutions, especially around the New Year. We post on Instagram the desires we have for ourselves in the next year, taking pictures of the food we eat and the smoothies we drink, hoping that the positive comments will continue to fuel us toward more self-care. And yet we are unsure of what self-care really looks like day in and day out.

Self-care is at the core of our desire to be healthy, to be whole, to feel connected. But within the ideas of self-care are layers and layers of privilege. What might be self-care for a middle-class woman in Beverly Hills is not self-care for a single mom in Chicago or a mother living on a reservation. Self-care is tricky, and we approach it with caution. Even so, it is necessary for the health and well-being of everyone that we practice self-care in the way that works for us.

In 2019 I spoke at a conference in Los Angeles called Publishing in Color, a gathering of authors and aspiring authors who meet with agents, editors, and published authors to move forward with their dreams of writing. I spoke that day on the power of self-care as a partner in the writing process. I talked about writing this book, how it required self-care day after day as I continued to write. I talked about how important it is for Black people, Indigenous people, and other people of color to have a community they can be safe with as they write about and process difficult things. Many of them told me they'd never heard a talk on self-care, which revealed the problem with our ideas of what self-care actually encompasses and how we so often tie it to shame and guilt. For Black people, Indigenous people, and people of color, it is especially difficult to approach the topic of self-care, because the system of self-care is often so unreachable for those who do not have the money to take care of themselves. There are many layers of privilege in the conversations, and self-care is often commodified, becoming yet another product of capitalism. When this happens, it also becomes harder for many of us to care for ourselves. We must consider all of this, and we must consider how our oppressive systems keep so many from getting the care they need. *Self-care is for everyone, to help us be more healthy humans,* but to get there, we all need to be honest about how the system of self-care works for all of us.

For me as an Indigenous woman, self-care looks like attending trauma therapy and knowing and loving myself both as the child I was and as the person I am in adulthood. It means setting boundaries and making space for stillness, and it has challenged me to step outside, to listen as the earth is speaking, to recognize the voice of sacred Mystery in the places I haven't before. Self-care means learning our Potawatomi language at home before I write. It means grounding myself in the deep well of goodness that flows out of culture and tradition and identity, the goodness that flows directly from the heart of Creator. Returning to my childhood memories can in itself be traumatic, and yet, looking back at myself, the ten-year-old Potawatomi girl who didn't understand the world around her except to look for God wherever God could be found, I hold grace now. I ask her to go easy, and I remind her that there is always grace without shame, there is always light and goodness waiting where the trees grow tall and the birds sing. Telling the truth is a tricky endeavor, and yet, it is a freeing one. Recognizing that my childhood was both beautiful and terribly painful is a truth I must face. Recognizing that the church is both full of beautiful people and yet terribly broken is a truth I have to reckon with. As Frederick Buechner once said, "Here is the world. Terrible and beautiful things will happen. Don't be afraid."[2]

For all of us to move toward healing together, we must walk through the fire, and we must be willing to stand beneath the trees and listen.

But before we can get there, many of us have to ask where we came from and who we are now, and this requires paying attention. How might we have conversations, even online, that create space for us to better care for ourselves and for one another? Yes, self-care is a constant journey to tether ourselves to what can heal us, but to get to healing, we have to acknowledge the wounds that put us here in the first place. We do that for ourselves individually, but we also do it together, remembering that our wholeness is connected to our belonging.

12

The Pain of Church Spaces

NOT LONG AFTER I started a job leading worship at a church in Atlanta, I attended a staff retreat at the Monastery of the Holy Spirit right outside town. It was the perfect location for a restful space to dream together. I was longing for the quiet, to have conversations that would foster community and encourage healthy identity-dynamics within the church. But it hadn't occurred to me that the weekend would also be incredibly confusing and emotionally fraught, as I began to process what it means to be a Potawatomi woman asking difficult questions about God and the institutional church.

One evening we attended a compline service together. The monks sang the Psalms and words of Jesus from the New Testament Gospels over us; it was a short service, but it felt like it lasted for hours. A few moments in, I began to weep. The heaviness of that moment, of listening to these religious men sing to and about God, became the tangible reminder that for generations, my own people were not allowed to sing to or about God in the way we were taught to honor *Kche Mnedo*, the Great Spirit, or *Mamogosnan*, Creator. Instead, we were taught to assimilate, to leave our identities behind and to become white people worshiping a white Jesus and an even whiter God. Suddenly, a holy place became a place wrapped up in pain, and I could hardly breathe.

The next day, I spoke with Brother Mark, one of the monks at the monastery. When I told him about my writing, he spoke about the wrongs done to Indigenous peoples and about how much respect he has for us. For just a moment, the juxtaposition of my deep pain and my deep gratitude for this man's words came together, and I saw once again that amid the really difficult work of truth-telling, we must also look for those who are already telling the truth. Monks and Native people have a few similar stereotypes told about us—in different ways, we are believed to be wise sages who spout life-giving sayings to anyone who interacts with us. That weekend, a monk and a Potawatomi woman converged in conversation, and it wasn't about who was wise or who knew God best; it was about two human beings seeing each other. We must look for those who are in the midst of arguments over church institutions and diversity, those who are already marching in the streets on behalf of the poor, those who *are the church* when so many of us don't even know who Jesus is anymore. Thich Nhat Hanh says in his book *Living Buddha, Living Christ*, "People kill and are killed because they cling too closely to their own beliefs and ideologies. When we believe that ours is the only faith that contains the truth, violence and suffering will surely be the result."[1] The problem isn't that we search for truth; the problem is that we become obsessed with our belief that we hold the truth, and we destroy entire cultures in the process. This is the tension I experience every time I walk into a church. Maybe we can learn to hold the truth that *Kche Mnedo, Mamogosnan*, the Great Spirit, Creator, or whatever name we give to that Divine Love, holds and loves us, and we are to love this earth we get to live on and to honor one another while we are here. "The true and essential work of all religion is to help us recognize and recover the divine image in everything," says Richard Rohr.[2]

I went back to that same monastery a few years later for a morning, just to write, think, and pray. This time I wasn't a worship leader at a church, wrestling with my identity in the world. This time I came as a woman, as a writer, as a seeker. I walked into the chapel praying that I might see and be seen—that the immigrants at the border might be seen, that those forgotten might be seen, that the hands of God, *Mamogosnan*, *Kche Mnedo*, might truly stretch wide enough to hold the pain of every century, the stain of every wrongdoing.

Is it possible?

I believe it is, and if it is, that means sacred love has always existed outside the church, outside the boxes we create with our cultural lenses, outside the distortions we put on that love.

Love must be timeless, expressed in all things, and if it is, that means it is the home we can always return to.

That means God is the Father and/or Mother who will always take us in.

That means, of course, we are never alone.

⸺❀⸺

Sometimes when we go to church on Sundays, I take my Citizen Potawatomi Nation coffee mug with me. I often wear my beaded earrings and a shirt that says *Phenomenally Indigenous* across the front. As I drink my coffee out of that mug and listen to the worship band play song after song, I begin to question things: Should I have left my *Nativeness* at the door? Should I stop bringing my Indigenous identity into a space that doesn't see or value it?

The white evangelical church in America has told us again and again that we must assimilate, that if we place our own "savage" identity alongside our faith, we are disgracing the gospel with our sin, we are idolaters who have no place in the church.

I grew up in a church culture that rewarded people pleasing, that punished those who asked too many questions, that pushed out those who seemed too angry or grieved too long. So as an adult, I'm finally asking all the questions I never asked when I was young. I'm wondering how, for all these years, the church has gotten away with so many oppressive acts toward women, Indigenous peoples, Black people, other people of color, disabled people, immigrants, those who journey with depression or anxiety, those who grieve, and those who are gender nonbinary, transgender, or queer. Can we go to church and be angry? Can we go to church and be *furious?* Can we go to church and ask questions? Can we go to church and fight against what we believe is wrong within it?

Absolutely.

Those of us who are angry cannot wait for the church to give us permission, because white supremacy will never give the oppressed permission to be angry. Barbara A. Holmes says in an essay on anger, "For people of color, anger wakes us up from our daze and desire to 'fit in,' no matter the cost."[3] When my anger finally woke me up, I realized that walking into church with my Potawatomi coffee mug is a small necessity. Asking questions is the thing that will keep me going, and my everyday reality is that anger and hope are colaborers, just as it is the reality for so many people who are trying to decolonize. For many, that anger led to movements like #emptythepews, a movement to encourage people to leave abusive church institutions, or #churchtoo, started by poet Emily Joy and Hannah Paasch, a movement that called out sexual abuse within churches against women and children—and for good reason. Many people are asking if the colonizer, institutional church can look any different than it has in the past. I believe that if it is ever going to look different, the church has to see its complicity in white supremacy throughout the centuries. It has to look at its own legacy, and it has to own that legacy. The American church must see that it has been partnered with capitalistic empire for far too long. The church must find a new way, or the anger that so many of us experience will go unseen and the church will continue to go unchecked.

The real question is this: Who gains life when we deconstruct these systems of whiteness, white supremacy, and toxic patriarchy? Everyone. Who loses out when we refuse to take a deep look at our own toxic systems? Everyone.

For the average, middle-class white person in church today, the lack of knowledge about our history of colonization within the walls of white American churches means that relationships that bring true, whole transformation are not available. Without these conversations, those people, those churches, and those institutions miss out on important opportunities for transformation. When we talk about decolonizing, we aren't just talking about wholeness for the oppressed or for Indigenous peoples. Ideas of equity and transparency will mark the path that leads to wholeness for all.

Power distorts the soul.

Empire distorts.

Oppression distorts.

Systems of whiteness distort.

The question is, How much do we want to see? Because once we see, we cannot un-see. Once we know, we cannot un-know.

The white church is afraid. But oh the liberation that waits on the other side of knowing! Oh the wholeness, the togetherness that comes with healing! This is the power of decolonizing. This is the grace that comes with *seeing*.

This is why the anger of Indigenous people, Black people, and other people of color is so important. It's why the anger of *women* is so important.

Something must change, and when it does, it will bring us all closer to our own humanity and to the holy mystery of God, a closeness only birthed through the journey of pain.

At some point, we learn how to please, and not how to *know*.

Glennon Doyle[4]

The church is made up of bodies. We tell metaphors about belonging to the body of Christ, we read Scripture passages like 1 Corinthians 12, about how we all belong to the one body but have separate roles, except that if you're a woman, suddenly your roles in the body become very specific: take care of the children, tend to the home, host potluck dinners, meet with other pastors' wives, host Bible studies for women only. So our roles within the church body become roles used by toxic patriarchy to protect itself, to control women and elevate the leadership of men.

In high school, I took part in the True Love Waits movement, gatherings where junior high and high school kids would come together to hear charismatic speakers talk about God's will (that we should wait until marriage to have sex). Speakers would then invite us to come forward and accept Jesus, accept the call to be pure and abstinent, or, even better, accept both. True Love Waits events were held at Memorial Hall in our small town, the auditorium packed with kids, their hormones soaring. The speakers always seemed to embody similar roles: The women told stories about how women are called to look after the men in our lives, to care for them, to wear clothing that doesn't tempt our brothers to lust, and to hold our virginity close until marriage because God asks us to, and when we get married, everything will seem to magically work just as it's supposed to because we will be *pure*. The men, on the other hand, told funny stories about puberty and the importance of being a *real man* in our society. Together, couples told their stories of how much it was worth it to wait to have sex until they were happily married. Basically, girls were told, again and again, to keep their breasts, shoulders, and legs covered so that the boys around us wouldn't be tempted by the lust that they are just naturally inclined toward, of no fault to them. Mix these experiences with those moments in my living room when I sat reading Joshua Harris's *I Kissed Dating Goodbye*, and so I had no intention of even *kissing* a boy until our wedding day. I wore my purity ring daily, the one toting a Scripture that says, "I am my beloved's and my beloved is mine" (Song of Songs 6:3).

On the day of my wedding shower, my best friends gave me lingerie—fairly modest, of course—that, at nineteen years of age, made me blush. The woman who hosted the shower, one of our youth group leaders, kindly reminded all of us that lingerie is for our husband, and that it is our job to wear it and to look nice for them, so that they, as men, are satisfied. I carried that into my marriage, just as the church told me to, so, I got married knowing nothing about my body or the vast, beautiful, and complex systems of sexuality we are born with. My identity was clouded by the idea of being *pure*, ironically the meaning of the name *Kaitlin*, so I carried that idea with me—and with it the false and toxic teachings that referred to women's bodies and spirits as something to be owned by God, the church, or our future husbands. *Be pure, because God is the King and you are his princess. Be pure, white as snow, because that's the best color of everything, but especially people.* Do you see how problematic this becomes? Our youth group also hosted princess conferences, girls-only weekends where we had modest-clothing fashion shows and did makeovers, pondering Bible verses about how God is the King and we are called to purity. In these spaces, I was instilling in myself a system of abstinence but of deep shame as well. In essence, I was being told that my white-passing, Christian body would be just as it needed to be as long as it was spotless and pure and willing to submit when the time came.

As an adult, I've begun exploring the rootedness of Indigenous feminism, which begins with the earth, *Segmekwe*, our mother. It is from her we learn what it means to be human, to be dependent on the things of the earth: the sun, the trees, the waters, the breezes, and the birds of the air. It is from her we learn what it means to be beautiful and to know beauty. Indigenous feminism flies in the face of everything I learned growing up by proclaiming that the bodies of Indigenous women cannot be overcome or controlled by systems of colonization, including the church. In this space, I learn what it means to be *kwe*, an Anishinaabe woman.

Native women have been through so much throughout history. We have lost our fathers and our brothers, our sisters and our mothers; we have faced abuse, rape, and murder and have held our families together. We have become social workers, water protectors, and community leaders; we have taken our work back to our people to support them, living in cities *and* outside them. We have held the fire when it has been most difficult. Anishinaabe author Leanne Betasamosake Simpson writes in her book *As We Have Always Done*, "Heteropatriarchy is not a discrimination that has come with white supremacy and colonialism; it is a *foundational dispossession force* because it is a direct attack on Indigenous bodies as political orders, thought, agency, self-determination, and freedom."[5]

Simpson's work helps directly tie Indigenous liberation of two-spirit people, queer people, children, and women to the political work we do every day to decenter colonization in our lives. To come out of the purity movement—a movement based largely in heteropatriarchy and misogyny—and to recognize the sacredness of my own feminine, *kwe* body, my own thoughts and experiences, has been a miraculous journey in and of itself, and I know I have so much more to learn.

We live in a society in which Indigenous women are targets of abuse—who go missing and are found murdered—and it is unnoticed by so much of the rest of society. Simpson calls out silence in the face of such injustice. "When we engage in gender violence or are silent in the face of homophobia, transphobia, heterosexism, discrimination, and ongoing gender violence, we are working in collusion with white men and on behalf of the settler colonial state to further destroy Indigenous nationhood."[6] We live in a patriarchal society, and church institutions are embedded in that society. Many of these institutions say women don't matter or that women simply exist for the pleasure of men, and within that system, Indigenous women, trans women, and women of color are treated even more unjustly. Nick Estes writes about the way fur traders dismantled matriarchal relations for Indigenous peoples, "which involved demanding the sexual services of Indigenous women's bodies—with or without their consent."[7] These attitudes and actions were part of creating an economy and culture based in both abuse and patriarchy, and it has formed everything that came after.

For a number of reasons, church spaces have become unsafe for so many people, and if we want to be honest about how that happened, we have to be honest about the origins of the colonizing, white American church, which was birthed out of European ways of knowing God and which used and still uses empire to get what it wants. The Doctrine of Discovery, conceived in and clarified over time by the church of Europe, gave European Christian men the power to overtake the people and the land in the Americas, which meant abuse of women and children in the process, abuse that continues today. Indigenous liberation and resistance are both ways of knowing who we are in the face of ongoing systems of oppression. For me, it means looking at my past, embedded in those systems, and holding up a mirror to the church today, empowering other women to do the same, just as they have empowered me.

If the church wants to be a safe space for anyone, it must begin with care for the most vulnerable, and if the church cannot be honest about the way it treats its most vulnerable, colonization will only continue to manifest itself within and outside church walls.

PART 3 SUMMARY

Truth is somehow both the work of uncovering what we didn't
know was there and the work of seeing what we knew was there
the whole time. Truth is taking off the bandage so the wound
can really heal. Often, it is the most painful possibility,
and yet, seeing the truth leads us to the good work
that waits for us, for the endless possibilities to create
what we did not know could be created. We searched,
we found truth, and now *we get to work*.

Working

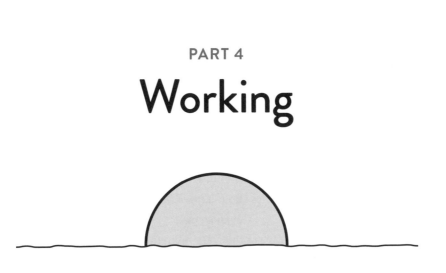

Original Man and all the animals were grateful.
They thanked muskrat and honored his life.
Turtle volunteered his shell so that they could see earth again.
They placed the dirt on his back and waited.
There, it grew . . .

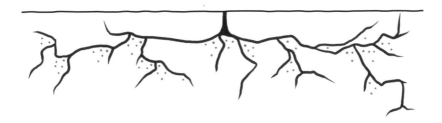

I am often in my own way.
Instead of experiencing
the Universe,
I write about experiencing
the Universe,
while at that very moment,
the wind had
holy secrets to tell me.

13

Wake-Up Calls

It is impossible to escape the sense that I am involved in history.

Wendell Berry, *Art of the Common Place*

WHEN THREATS to the Dakota Access Pipeline in Standing Rock, North Dakota, became a national story in 2016, it was the first time I experienced, in a way I could name, the heaviness of intergenerational trauma that goes along with settler colonialism and erasure. Indigenous peoples carry this trauma our whole lives but often in ways we cannot name, because trauma is something that doesn't always reveal itself in ways we would expect. Standing Rock helped crack open something that had been buried deep inside me. Nick Estes, in his book *Our History Is the Future*, writes, "Indigenous resistance is not a one-time event. It continually asks: What proliferates in the absence of empire? Thus, it defines freedom not as the absence of settler colonialism, but as the amplified presence of Indigenous life and just relations with human and nonhuman relatives, and with the earth."[1] Throughout US history, this has guided the interactions between oppressor and oppressed, and we saw it happening in real time as news broadcasters like Democracy Now! put their feet on the ground to bear witness and stand watch. There was no other way America would have known that people who supported the pipeline were releasing attack dogs on Indigenous water protectors and their allies. There is no other way America would have known that the police department was working with military gear when they should have been protecting the land and the people from corporations that were seeking to destroy them.

Every day I would sit on our living room couch and watch live streams, from my phone, from my laptop—horrified, surprised, but also coming alive to the realization that it has always been this way. History herself was coming to tell me that I belong to her, that I belong to all these stories that have been covered up in dust, covered up by whiteness. For the first time I connected within my own experiences what it was like to face oppression, but I also understood that I was held secure within a spiritual and political movement that was carrying us all, a movement that had carried our ancestors. The truth is, the water protectors had voices, and they were using them. I thought about our tribe's prophecies, a vision of a time when young people will return to learn our Indigenous ways and reignite the fires of our cultures and traditions.

We live in a time of great resistance, of prayerful nonviolence, a time of young people calling out to others to join them in a new movement in the midst of settlers who "imagined building a pipeline in a world where Native people did not exist."[2]

Native peoples who stand up for their identity and for the land have always been met with violence, suppression, and aggression from white people. This is the legacy of white supremacy, and it has never gone away. Since Standing Rock, America has been more aware of Indigenous voices, much like the rise of resistance and Indigenous voices in the 1960s and '70s with AIM, the American Indian Movement. Though we have been speaking, resisting, engaging in important conversations and partnerships, and remembering who we are in the face of oppression, Indigenous youth are still rising up to speak, Native writers and artists are sharing their work, women are sharing about our responsibility to care for the earth. We have always been here, and yet, sometimes you need organizations like Democracy Now! to remind the rest of society that we did not die in the old Westerns you used to watch on television, and our cultures did not disappear despite boarding schools. We are still here. We are still creating, and our children are leading us into a new generation, all over the world fighting pipeline after pipeline and injustice after injustice. They are the Indigenous resistance the world is so hungry for. Standing Rock would not let us ignore it then, and it will not let us forget now.

The struggle at Standing Rock is not over, even though the crowds have left. Pipelines across Turtle Island, like the Trans Mountain Pipeline approved by both President Trump and Prime Minister Trudeau, continue to threaten the lives of Indigenous people and the well-being of our societies. So, the wake-up call to use our voices, whether we are Native or not, is one we cannot ignore.

⸱—❀—⸱

One fall Saturday morning, I went to a lake near our house to work and write. I'd spent so much time inside, at coffee shops and sitting at my office desk, that I felt like I couldn't write what needed to come out of me anymore. It was like I was paralyzed by a low buzz, by bright lights and constant movement, by the presence of the internet. So I put some coffee in a thermos, grabbed my black thin-point Sharpie, notebook, and laptop, and headed out. There is a one-way covered bridge on the way to the lake, and as I passed it, I saw fog rolling on top of the water, welcoming me. All my defenses fell away; I took a deep breath and let the world speak.

When those water protectors gathered to pray and resist, *Segmekwe* listened and spoke back. She shared about the wounds she'd been enduring over time, and about the things she'd seen. The Oceti Sakowin of that place were the ones listening to her, trying to keep her safe, honoring her stories. So it is with this lake and this land only twenty minutes from my home. It has endured destruction and construction, its mountains blasted for granite in the late 1800s. It is sore, and yet it teaches me. The fog reminds me that quiet voices still speak. The acorns falling from the tops of the trees remind me that gravity is meant to ground us and sustain us here. The birds, arguing in the sky over who wants to fly where, remind me that my angle of seeing is limited, that I am small. The dying autumn leaves remind me that it is part of life to die and live again, that death itself can somehow be beautiful. And the rocks and dirt at my feet remind me that though they are sore, they still have something to say to me, just like they had something to say to the people who came before in this place, the Muscogee Creek and Cherokee people who once walked this land.

I remembered the day I took my boys to the Standing Rock protest in downtown Atlanta. I strapped my guitar to my back in case we needed to sing, and my boys marched through the downtown streets alongside me and all the other protestors, yelling, "Water is life!"

It was my first protest, and it was the first protest for my two sons, then three and five years old, who were witnessing what it means to have a collective voice and to let that voice be heard. On those streets, marching with others, I knew the future is the children and that "the answers lie within the kinship relations between Indigenous and non-Indigenous and the lands we both inhabit."[3] I saw a Palestinian man marching with us that day, and as we passed by him, he just nodded and said, "I know what you're going through. I stand with you." I know that for the Pot-awatomi spirit to continue to burn brightly, our children must carry the flame into the next generation, and that if we let them, they will. But we must listen to the quiet and steady voice of the earth to guide us, standing in solidarity with one another as we do so. We must hear the creatures that have inhabited these spaces since the beginning of time. We must remember that they are our teachers, or we will never learn anything about ourselves. If it is not because of a pipeline, it will be because of something else, some other threat to the very life of *Segmekwe*. The work of the people, the organic, grassroots, feet-on-the-ground work, cannot come just from the Indigenous people of the land. It must reach across cultures, socioeconomic status, and skin color. We must all work together, Native and non-Native, to fulfill prophesies that call people back to unity, that call healing back over the land, that listen to her as she tells us that though she is sore, she is still speaking, that though she is bruised, she will still wake us up and heal us.

⌁—✦—⌁

My dear friend Idelette gifted me a coffee mug, made by artist Emily McDowell, that says, "Give me a refill. The patriarchy isn't going to fight itself." I use this mug often, not because fighting against patriarchy is a fun trend that is going to disappear but because it reminds me that the books I am writing and the words I am speaking are for the purpose of bringing peace. And to bring peace to those who have been oppressed means that my words must break down systems of toxic patriarchy on a deep and holy level. It reminds me that this is about more than a women's march, more than attending a protest, more than a bio tagline that says "activist."

It's about a lived experience and a willingness to step into the difficult spaces and speak the truth, to listen to the prophets of our day who speak out against systems of abuse that take up space all over the world. Richard Wagamese once wrote, "To seek harmony is to seek truth, and truth seekers have always had a rough go of it in the world."[4]

Fighting against toxic patriarchy has been a hot topic for a few years now as marches and protests (often led by women of color) have increased in response to the Trump administration, and it's easy to get wrapped up in *smashing the patriarchy* without realizing what doing so might cost some of us. Trump's time as president has been marked by numerous accounts of women who have come forward with allegations that he sexually assaulted or even raped them, and the response of the president is always to make a mockery of these women and to brag, once again, that as a powerful man in this nation (and now the most powerful man in the world), he can do as he pleases. Threatening patriarchy is a dangerous thing, and the people who suffer most from it are those on the margins, those who have always been at the bottom of the social pyramid, while those holding up the patriarchy keep comfortable with their power at the top. While those at the bottom suffer, though, I think that the ones who have benefited from its power so much—like evangelical white women, for example—fear losing what power they've gained in upholding patriarchy.

This is why Trump has so many female supporters. This is why women of color talk about the struggle against white women, and I've seen this played out in the church a lot. *Women oppress other women because patriarchy rewards those who follow the rules.*

As a white-coded woman, I have been given many opportunities as a worship leader in the church, and yet, because I am also an Indigenous woman, I am a threat to a system of whiteness that is entrenched in patriarchy. Though I am treated with respect as a leader, when I speak about being Indigenous and about our rights within an abusive system of government and church, I am seen as someone who might cause a stir, someone who perhaps confronts issues that have been present and ignored for a long time. But this is not just my experience. Many people end up on the outside of religious institutions: disabled people, people of color, minority communities, LGBTQ+ folks—they are shining that light on patriarchal systems and asking if this is really what love is all about, if this is really how people should be treated. For those who have held the power, breaking systems of patriarchy can be scary. But in the end, it benefits everyone because it allows all voices to be heard and valued for who they are and what they have to give. We are watching this happen with Congresswoman Alexandria Ocasio-Cortez and other congresswomen who are dismantling the patriarchal systems of America by shining a light on how much power many generations of white men have held in the White House. And what we have to realize is that breaking down systems of toxic patriarchy is lifelong work, work for men, women, and those who identify as nonbinary. It's a relay race, it's a pass-the-baton kind of race in which we learn what we need to do in our generation and we let the children of the next generation lead in whatever ways they must lead. According to Amnesty International UK, Indigenous rights activism is considered one of the top six most dangerous kinds of activism, and that is because going up against settler colonial systems means going up against powerful systems of patriarchy that have created the US as it is today.[5] So fighting against pipelines and speaking up for Indigenous rights is a lot more dangerous than many think it is, and we have to understand that we fight it now so that later our children know that what we stood for matters. We wake ourselves up to today's realities so that our children know what they will face for their generation. Our work cannot be a fad. It is a constant wake-up call, echoed throughout history. It is a constant question of what our future work must be in order for it to be enough to change things. I believe we are enough and we can change things. I believe toxic systems will crumble beneath the glorious weight of world-rattling, inclusive joy—but to get there, the church has a lot of work to do.

14

When the Church Gets to Work

WHEN I WAS IN SIXTH GRADE, I did a long project on Sojourner Truth, born Isabella Baumfree, a Black woman who was enslaved from birth, freed herself, and became a women's rights activist and abolitionist. Isabella changed her name to Sojourner Truth when she embarked on the journey of abolition. Since I was in sixth grade, Truth has returned to inspire and compel me throughout my life, reminding me what it means to work against systems that oppress. Her story and the stories of others are still leading the church to ask new, difficult questions and to make room at the table for those who have long been left out.

When the church gets to work, conferences that were once only for white, evangelical audiences and led by white men become conferences where diverse audiences show up and see themselves represented on the stage and feel that they can truly show up as they are. This has come after years of struggle, years of women pushing and pushing for representation within the church. Still, these conferences are few and far between, and to continue in a better direction requires a lot of work on all sides.

For the church to truly do the work it is called to do, that representation must not be simply a form of tokenism, a chance to get a Native American speaker in the doors so you can say you did an important and trendy thing once. The path of Sojourner Truth requires more of us, and if we are willing to follow, the landscape of the American church should look different.

One weekend a few years ago I attended a conference in Tennessee for church and worship leaders. The audience and speakers at the conference were mostly white, sprinkled with a few Black people and one Native woman (me). That weekend, I decided that I didn't really want anyone to know I was Potawatomi. I wanted to blend into the crowd and not have awkward conversations. I would just be the worship leader me and let the other aspects of my identity come out as they needed to. In other words, I wanted to compartmentalize.

That first evening, as Brian McLaren began to speak, I saw the direction the conference was turning. The conference leaders admitted to us early on that their dream for future conferences was to have more people of color as speakers and attendees, that they were disappointed they couldn't be more successful in that goal. Their honesty was rooted in a desire to make the church better than it is, and I was grateful for that, but I also recognized that in so many church conference spaces, organizers *must work harder* to bring in leaders of color and to pay them for their work. Brian's talk that evening was on the Doctrine of Discovery, in which Columbus and those who came after him were given authority "under God," by the church, to take control and possession of any land deemed "not Christian" and do whatever was necessary to conquer the land and the people already living there. He spoke on the difficult reality that if the church truly wants to become more inclusive, it has to face its past, its complicity and silence in the oppression, genocide, and removal of Indigenous peoples throughout history, all over the earth, but specifically in North America. I sat, overwhelmed, through the entire presentation, because I wasn't ready for this. I had been compartmentalizing, keeping that part of my identity out of the picture for a weekend. But here I was, being called back into it, being told, *This is who you are. Speak from it.*

The last morning of the conference, one of the conference leaders, Bryan Sirchio, shared what he learned about Indigenous peoples and the church's role in our suffering. He shifted the worship of the morning to focus on that, to pray and think about how the church can make space to truly grieve its complicity. As I drove back to Atlanta when the conference was over, I held renewed hope that for the church to become better than what it has been, I must be *all that I am*, someone who jumps into difficult conversations because they are necessary. I must be part of the work, part of the questions, and part of the solutions.

The sixth-grade version of me did this when she stood in front of a crowd to bear witness to the life and story of Sojourner Truth, and as an adult, I am still bearing witness, not only to my own story but to the story of a Christianity that is learning to face its own demons.

I have attended many events focused on justice for the oppressed. I have attended conferences around the country and have been invited to share my story. It is strange to be someone who is tokenized, and yet, I have come to the conclusion that if none of us are invited to the table, the stories of Indigenous peoples will never be told. If I come and share my own experiences as a Potawatomi woman, I might pave the way for other conversations to happen, for other Indigenous speakers to show up and share their stories. As I speak and as I deal with all the uncomfortable conversations that come with it, I realize in conversations the deep ignorance many Americans have when it comes to Indigenous existence and identity in the world.

As Christians in America, we so often want a quick and easy fix, an answer that we can put in our back pocket to pull out when things get tough. But that's not how it works, especially when it comes to groups the church has oppressed. Numerous people have approached me after speaking events wanting to know how to build relationships with Indigenous peoples for the sake of their churches.

But this is altogether missing the point.

As Indigenous peoples, we cannot give the church all the answers that the church wants, and the answers we *do give* may not be what the church is expecting. We are existing and resisting in a settler colonial society that has been set up to destroy who we are, and it is the job of the white American church to listen, to respect, to mourn when it's time to mourn, and to learn when it's time to learn on their own terms without demanding that Black people, Indigenous people, and other people of color be constant educators.

Approaching Indigenous culture with the goal of getting Native peoples in the pews isn't an answer—it is merely an extension of colonization. Perhaps the church should consider that Indigenous peoples have more to teach the church than the church has to teach Indigenous peoples. Perhaps that would change how the relationship works. The important aspect of this relationship is that it is a partnership, a space in which listening really happens, a space in which Indigenous people are paid for their time and resources by the church itself, if asked. As I said earlier, Indigenous people shouldn't have to spend our days educating non-Native people, but when we are willing to partner with institutions like the church for a better future, we should be heard. I respect my Indigenous relatives who will never step foot in a church because of all the harm that has been done to our ancestors, and on this side of things, I want to be part of conversations that will hopefully foster change and help dismantle those toxic and oppressive systems.

Many justice efforts I've witnessed work hard to combat systems of oppression in America and around the world but are still leaving out the horrible effects colonization and oppression have on Indigenous populations. We talk about the importance of adoption, but we don't mention that Indigenous children are forcefully taken from their Indigenous families without consent and adopted into white families, not just throughout history but still today. We talk about violence against women of color, but we don't say anything about missing and murdered Indigenous women, whose families must decide whether they can trust the government to seek justice for their sisters, daughters, grandmothers, and aunties. We talk about police brutality, but we don't mention that Native Americans are killed by law enforcement at a higher rate than any other racial group in the US.[1] If the church really wants to get to work to face the injustices of our time, the church cannot ignore the injustices against Indigenous peoples that have been happening since before the birth of this nation.

I once asked my seven-year-old son what he loves about being Potawatomi, and he said that while he loves learning our stories and who we are, it is sad to know that so many bad things have happened to us. In essence, my seven-year-old is saying that to understand what it means to be Potawatomi in America, we also have to understand what has been done to us historically and what is still done to us today. If he cannot step into faith spaces and ask these questions and process his own identity, how will any of us be able to process who we are and what it means to live in America today? If pastors and conferences can't make room for lament, for grief, for honest conversations, for inclusion of the Indigenous experience, how will we ever move forward? Healing must happen for all of us, or it cannot happen at all.

So, my hope rests with those who are having the hard conversations, who are leaning in to do the work. It's with the people who are supporting Indigenous artists, who are giving support by backing our work and making sure that we know we matter in the world. If the church cannot be an institution that supports and lifts up the people outside itself, it will further lose its own identity in the process.

◦—❀—◦

We spend a lot of time, especially on social media, pointing out the people we think are getting it wrong, the ones who lead and contribute to oppressive ideas and systems. But we don't always point out our allies, the friends who join us in the work of wholeness and love. When I was writing my first book and trying to navigate the world of being an author in the twenty-first century, one of the people who first came alongside me in the church, encouraging me as a writer and believing in me as a human being, was Rachel Held Evans. And Rachel didn't just believe in me as a woman or as a writer, but she constantly lifted me up as a *Potawatomi* woman. She acknowledged and respected my identity from the beginning, and because of her, I knew there was still a church worth fighting for.

We quickly became friends after we met at the Why Christian? conference, created by Rachel and Nadia Bolz-Weber. At the conference, a number of us gathered on a stage at Duke University's chapel to answer this question: Why am I still a Christian? There is no simple answer, and Rachel and Nadia both knew that. Over the course of the weekend, Rachel and I would find ourselves huddled in a corner, laughing about our hilariously similar conservative upbringings and our proclivity to count how many souls we thought we'd saved by high school. We were friends who wrote side by side, and friends who dreamed together.

In April 2019, Rachel was hospitalized for the flu, and more complications continued to emerge. After being in an induced coma, Rachel died on May 4, 2019. Christianity lost one of its leaders and prophets, and I lost one of my dearest friends. Rachel was someone who challenged a seemingly set-in-stone world of

Christianity to ask how it treats its most vulnerable: women, people of color, LGBTQ+ people, disabled people, and children, among others. Rachel asked if we read the Bible the way we *should* read it, and helped us come to the conclusion that God is always bigger and love is always wider than we'd imagined.

Measuring the ripple effects of goodness Rachel left in the world seems impossible, but our *individual* stories bear witness to the gifts she gave and continues to give us. The week she died made that very clear, as people who knew her personally and those who didn't flocked to social media sites to pay homage, to share stories, and to say, "I'm here today because of Rachel."

I met Rachel a few years into the process of deconstructing my own Christian faith, at a critical time in my life when church and community were difficult to come by. This woman who had led so many others to a vision of an inclusive church was taking a chance on me, and I wasn't sure why.

Rachel not only read my words and told me that they mattered; she also took my hand and led me to a Christianity that I did not know existed, one that included all the questions I had and the ones I didn't even know were coming yet. She showed me that when the church gets to work, good things happen, and we find healing.

Rachel led me to more questions.

Rachel led me to a deeper faith.

Rachel led me to friendship and laughter.

Rachel led me to dreams for a better future of the church.

Rachel led me back to myself.

But the truth is, Rachel wasn't just a leader.

She was a *reach-across-the-table-and-build-something-new-together* visionary.

Because of Rachel, I've found a community of people who have chosen, like she did, to see and value my voice in the world. I've met people who are walking alongside me, asking how they can support Indigenous peoples better, asking how they can tell the truth to their own children and their own communities.

In 2018, at the inaugural Evolving Faith conference that Rachel hosted with Sarah Bessey, we saw again how Rachel could bring people from varying backgrounds together to ask, "Why are we here, and how can we help each other?" Through stories and convictions, through questions and sometimes shrugging shoulders, we stood on that stage to join together in the acknowledgment that as humans, we are people who are constantly transforming, *evolving*, and that we have to stick together in that work. Rachel knew that, and that's what made her the advocate she was.

After she died, people began to ask, "What now? Who will speak? Who will guide us and lead us, and who will make the table bigger?" It seems that what Rachel might want is that each of us finds exactly how we do that in our own unique way, in a way that leads others toward a more inclusive kind of love and to a bigger table where we can sit together and share our stories, where we can find the very sacredness of God in one another and in the world outside us.

When we lose a prophet, it shakes the foundations of everything we know to be true. We feel afraid because we've lost a guiding voice, and we feel empowered to carry on their work because they asked us to. But when a friend dies, the foundations don't just shake; they split into pieces and everything seems to fall apart until it can slowly be put back together again.

When I'm not sure how I will do anything without her, I imagine her there, taking my hand and saying in that warm, Southern voice, "Oh, you've got this!"

That's Rachel. It was always Rachel, and it will always be Rachel. We must courageously pick up her fierce love and carry it with us into a church that in many ways is still waiting for healing.

15

Keeping Watch

THE DAY THAT TAHLEQUAH'S CALF DIED, I had no idea. It wasn't like the foundations of the earth shook, telling me that a mother orca whale in Puget Sound was grieving. I saw it on the news a few days later, but once I knew, Tahlequah's presence wouldn't leave my mind.

Through her grief, we were all trying to learn something. It had never been recorded that a whale had carried their deceased baby that long. For seventeen lingering days, her pod alongside her, she wailed in the way only an orca can. They were in communal mourning, and I couldn't help but ask if humans even know how to mourn anymore. A few months before this, I had started trauma therapy, and I was learning that often we don't know how to name things.

Grief.
Trauma.
Joy.
Loneliness.
Community.
Anger.
Abandonment.

Mystery.
Misery.
Sacredness.
Self-care.

We like to throw these words around for other people to use, but when they bubble up inside us, we don't know what to say or how to act on them, what to *name*. I was watching an orca whale mourn more in seventeen days than I'd mourned anything in twenty years. Beyond that, my mourning and Tahlequah's mourning were connected. Humanity takes what it wants, when it wants it. Dams and pollution are killing off salmon, endangering orca whale populations, endangering the water, the thing we call sacred, the thing we're tasked to protect.

So as Tahlequah grieved, I couldn't help but ask how much of her grief resulted from humanity's mistakes, greed, capitalism, lack of care, and heartlessness. It is the lie, since the beginning, that we are made to be alone. We are not only made for community within our own species—we belong to all the creatures of the earth, our kin.

In *The Mishomis Book* by Edward Benton-Banai, we learn the story of Original Man and the wolf. Unlike the Hebrew story in which Adam is given Eve as a companion, Original Man is given the wolf as a partner to walk the earth. They keep watch together. They care for the creatures they encounter *together*. If we are people called to keep watch, that means we are people called to keep care, to pay attention. It is about more than just recycling; it is about a stance toward the earth of humility and eagerness to learn, because everything around us has a story to tell and a sacred life to be lived.

In the Baptist church I grew up in, the only time I heard anything about the earth was when a preacher talked about our call to "subdue" it (Genesis 1:28), interpreted as "take what you want because you're human and don't worry about the effects of your selfishness and abuse of power." In this show of arrogance, we see an attitude of white supremacy that has existed since the beginning of America, as Christians have desecrated the land in the name of God. In the midst of it, Indigenous peoples have been leaders in caring for *Segmekwe*, and if the church wants to find a new way to exist in an era of climate change conversations, it needs to put worldwide Indigenous voices first.

It will take more than a flannelgraph in a Sunday school class-room to change the future and prepare our children for what it will mean for them to face climate change. We cannot have these discussions within our faith spaces without being honest about our complicity. We know that oppressed people, the poor, people of color, and Indigenous communities suffer far greater from the effects of climate change than privileged, white communities, because cycles of oppression last for generations, trapping people in poverty in their own communities. If we start out poor, when the effects of climate change begin to worsen, they will hit us in ways that privileged communities will not suffer. So, the poor get poorer, and those who were already struggling with health are going to get sicker, and our healthcare system will not care for them. If we cannot help our children understand this, we are not preparing them to be people who *watch and pay attention*. If we cannot help our children understand why the life of an orca whale matters, we will have a hard time showing them why love birthed in the mystery of God matters.

In Potawatomi culture, it is in the wintertime that we tell stories while the world sleeps, while the animals hibernate for a few months. It is the time of our elders, a time we gather around them to listen, to take in the words that have carried our people for generations. It is the time for our children to learn where we come from and to dream about where we are going.

We need to keep telling Tahlequah's story. We need to keep telling the stories of creation, the stories of Original Man and the wolf, stories of our dependence on and partnership with the earth and all creatures in it. Otherwise, we won't know how to mourn. We won't know how to be human. We won't know *how to love.*

As a white-coded Potawatomi woman, someone who is a citizen of both the US and the Potawatomi nation, I have a lot to watch for. I must watch my own privilege, afforded to me by the color of my skin. I must watch for injustices done against my Indigenous kin all over the world, and I must watch for microaggressions—the subtle actions or statements, often unintentional, that are spoken against members of marginalized groups every day. We must constantly be on watch, because we don't know who we can trust. We don't know what kinds of interactions we will have with others on a daily basis when we talk about being Indigenous.

"So, how much Native blood do you have?"

"You don't look like an Indian."

"Oh! My Grandma was full-blooded Cherokee."

"Wow, I've never met a Native American before!"

"Yes, you have dark hair and high cheekbones, just like those other Indian women."

These are microaggressions that any number of Native peoples have heard often throughout our lives, and they are based on dangerous stereotypes and narratives that have been carried down for generations in America. The presumption that everyone living in the southeast or in Oklahoma has a Cherokee grandma is a problem. The presumption that we can cut our bodies into sections to find out how Native we are through the atrocious idea of "blood quantum" is a problem. The idea of the blood quantum was created in order to eventually let Native blood "run out," so that we would no longer exist as Indigenous people but be completely assimilated into whiteness and unable to participate as citizens of our tribes. And the presumption that most people haven't ever met a Native person before is terribly damaging, because Indigenous peoples live all over the country, on reservations and in cities, in rural spaces and even in the suburbs. So, keeping watch has to be the work of all of us, on a collective level.

I commonly see progressive Christians come alongside people of color as advocates, demonizing conservatives, the "other side," for atrocities "they" have committed, while neglecting to notice that they themselves also play a part in the narrative and work of settler colonialism. We saw this in the liberals who jumped to defend Elizabeth Warren when some Indigenous peoples (Cherokee people and their allies) called her out for sharing the results of a DNA test to "prove" that she is Cherokee. To call out the racism of President Trump, they ignored the ways Warren encouraged racist stereotypes by taking a DNA test and using Indigenous identity for her own gain. I am not saying that Trump and Warren are the same; but I am saying we need to be careful about how much we demonize one another over things we do not understand, or we risk becoming the very thing we are so sure we are fighting against.

These situations do not help us work toward decolonizing anything but continue to build our history on lies passed down from us to our children and on to our grandchildren. Where will we break the narrative? We must acknowledge that white supremacy runs through the veins of all American enterprises, institutions, and systems, and for that to be understood, there is work to be done on all sides.

My friend and fellow writer Jeff Chu recently graduated from the Farminary, a project at Princeton Theological Seminary that strives to connect theology with agriculture and creation care. While working there, Jeff spent his days with words, with worms and compost, watching plants come up from the ground. He spent his days *paying attention*, because that is what gardeners must do, what keepers of the earth must do.

The ancestors of Potawatomi people were people who watched. They watched for winter to come, the time to tell our stories, to gather in, the elders' time. They watched the maple trees for the time to make syrup. They watched the moon for its cycles. They watched the fires, tending to them, *keepers of the fire*, just as we continue to do today. We watch our own fires, we tend to our own narratives, and we watch what is happening around us. We care for this earth, for the compost and the worms, for the ants and the basil growing outside our front door. To be someone who *watches* is to be someone who pays attention.

In the church, white people are often the ones who have the privilege of stepping in and out of this work of paying attention. Conferences put a few people of color as speakers on the stage before a white audience, and that audience gets to *watch* and take what they saw home with them. It's compelling, it's energizing, but it's also dangerous. The work of watching can end up centering whiteness, and so if we want to talk about the church's responsibility to be people who *watch*, the church has to be willing to allow the people who lead and keep watch to be Black people, Indigenous people, and other people of color. The leaders should be women, immigrants, trans people, queer people, disabled people, and children. Those who keep watch are the ones that no one expects; they are the ones who come with stories to tell because they keep their ears tuned to the mysteries of this world, to the magic of God in her many subversive forms. So, like Jeff, we keep watch. We look at layers of compost and see miracles. We look at worms and see keepers of sacredness, finding what is holy where we least expected it.

❧

One Southern winter a few years ago, the weather became cold enough to freeze everything around us. So we traveled to Tennessee for a day, to spend an afternoon exploring outside the city with our dogs and our two sons. We hiked down a steep path of tree branches, roots, and rocks until we came to an open space with a magnificently powerful waterfall. The force of the water had broken through the ice beneath it, and I stood there watching stream after engulfing stream plunge itself over the cliff above into the pool below. In the middle, the ice had given way for the water, but all around that area everything stayed frozen, immovable. I imagined the steady, engulfing power of mystery that breaks through our hardened places, to destroy the roots of corruption in us. I watched, and the water would not relent. I watched, remembering that gravity does not give up its power to anyone else on this earth.

Part of working toward a better world, and working toward a better church, is recognizing that if we tether ourselves to the messy reality of Jesus, a man who lived in the middle of thousands of tensions every day, we must be honest about our own hard and soft places. And this isn't just our individual ideas of sin and salvation—this is the collective and *communal* work of righting the wrongs that have been created in the wake of empirical American Christianity. Brené Brown, in her book *Rising Strong*, wrote about a moment when her therapist Diana said to her, "Yes. I really do believe that most of us are doing the very best we can with the tools we have."[1] So what tools are we using, and how do we practice love?

While the above statement is true, it isn't an excuse for abuse and oppression. Instead, it is an invitation to enter into the work of truth-telling, of *keeping watch*, of being people who will ask hard questions and hold grace in the difficult spaces. Even in an era of the white, American, evangelical church struggling to know itself and face its demons, we hold these institutions accountable for the harm they inflict—*and* we keep our own hearts soft in the process. We garden. We visit waterfalls. We listen to trees speak. We feel the wind on our face. We return to the earth as she heals us, as God heals us, and then we do the hard work. We watch, and then we work. We watch, and then we act.

And when we act, it can be difficult. It is difficult to call these toxic systems out when the time is right. It can be difficult to say out loud, *Yes, my ancestors and yours were racist, and we have to ask what that means for us today.* Or, *Yes, the foundations of this church are steeped in white supremacy.* In the midst of making mistakes, we have to learn how to handle them, how to learn from them.

I have watched friends who are people of color call out the white allies in their lives, and I have watched those white allies get defensive, shouting, "I am not racist! How dare you accuse me of being a white supremacist!" The truth is, our complicity in racism and white supremacy speaks to the systems we have created as a whole. It isn't just KKK leaders who are fueled by white supremacy; white supremacy is subtle, buried deep inside the psyche of American ideals, and those are the ideals we must also confront. Yes, it is an individual critique, and Black people, Indigenous people, and other people of color are asking that the world receive that critique. Disabled people are asking to be seen and respected in their bodies, and we should be listening. Our LGBTQ+ friends are wondering who will speak when churches silence them and their own families abandon them. Immigrant families are wondering who will stand against ICE raids to protect their children. We must *act*, because too many systems have kept oppression spinning relentlessly, and if we cannot band together to stop it, no one will.

It is not solely the job of the oppressed to break apart toxic systems; the privileged must partner with the oppressed and come together with their own tools to fix what is broken. In the process, it will require the privileged to give up some of that privilege. Archbishop Desmond Tutu and the Dalai Lama talk about the power of joy in *The Book of Joy: Lasting Happiness in a Changing World.* In a world in which it is easier to ignore and avoid pain, we must lean into it to truly find joy, just as both these men have done. In a similar way, we cannot ignore the injustices of our time, but, together, we must lean into honest conversations so that together we can move forward, toward healing, toward joy. *That* is the work of watching, the work of waiting, the work of acting. As Thomas Merton says, "Love cannot come of emptiness. It is full of reality."[2]

16

Fighting Invisibility

THE YEAR MY FIRST BOOK CAME OUT, I attended a book club with a friend's church. A small group of women had been studying my book, and I was an honored guest one quiet Saturday morning. I arrived to find a table full of snacks and fresh coffee, and women seated in a circle in a cozy living room. I sat in a corner chair, huddled up and ready for a conversation.

The women went around the room sharing what my book meant to them, and what struck me most was the reaction of a young woman named Alicia, who is mixed race/culture/ethnicity. In essence, she told me that the book brought up hard things. With a sly smirk and a serious tone, she was mirroring exactly what I have been experiencing over the last few years: a painful journey to discover identity, to name whiteness, and to claim all that we are in those complex spaces. It is painful and necessary, and once we begin, there is no turning back. In my own mixed identity of being an Indigenous woman and a Christian, a descendent of European people but also belonging to my tribe, I struggle with what it means to belong in many spaces, how to acknowledge my own *whiteness*, how to fight against its implications in the world and how to use it to dismantle systems of hate.

Not long after I left that day, I wrote Alicia a letter, one that I hope resonates with anyone who is biracial, multiracial, multiethnic, mixed race, mixed ethnicity, or mixed culture. There are many people, in-between people, who walk in liminal spaces with an acknowledgment that all of life is a complex struggle, but one we should not handle alone. This letter is for all of you too.

Dear Alicia,

I met you at a book club. You'd just read my first book, and you told me that it woke something up in you. You told me that you don't know how to walk the hard road of being mixed, that you know it's going to be hard, and that you don't know what it will look like.

I liked you right away.

I have noticed throughout my life that I am someone who lives in constant tension, a person who lives in gray spaces. When I met you, I knew I wasn't alone.

Do you know that there are a lot of us? There are a lot of people walking a complicated journey, people with mixed heritage, races, ethnicities, cultures.

They are asking what it means to be faithful in all things.

They are asking if it's possible to live a decolonized life.

They are asking if whiteness really has the last word.

They are asking if the American church really has any room for them.

Alicia, I have dreams.

I dream of being someone who meets more people like us and calls out that which has long been forgotten, suppressed, and beaten down by cultures and systems of whiteness. I dream of saying to the mixed people in the room, "You are enough. Give voice to that sacredness inside you that has long been told to be quiet." We are the ones who are told to be one thing or the other thing, to choose *because we can't possibly inhabit more than one space at a time. We are told not to take up too much room at the table, because there's barely enough room for us—unless it can fully represent wanted whiteness.*

Hear me on this. *Speaking into these spaces will cost us something. It will mean that we choose to forsake the call of assimilation, the pressure to pursue whiteness. It will mean that we are told we are* too much *and that we should* calm down *and that we make people* uncomfortable.

And yet, we should speak and move and breathe from the spaces within us that are asking to be given a voice. We can learn the languages and ways of our ancestors, we can embrace our otherness *until it becomes the thing that guides us all.*

Do not be afraid, but be empowered.

We will fight together.

We will dream together.

We will remember together.

And when it's hard, we will love ourselves—together.

Friend, don't lose hope.

Hope is the thing that will lead us.

> *Love,*
> *Kaitlin*

❧—✿—❧

For the past two years, I have been traveling with my tribal ID, because, according to TSA guidelines, it is a valid form of identification when going through security at an airport. I began traveling independently when I was twenty-eight, when I first got the opportunity to travel around the country and speak on faith in everyday life and my experience as a Potawatomi woman. Before that, I never thought about using my tribal ID until I realized how important it would be, both for me and for the people around me.

So, I prepare. I take extra time to travel through the line and security, because I do not know if I will be detained, or if it will take an hour for the TSA agents to recognize my identity as valid. When I arrive at the airport, and as I move up the line, getting closer to that little desk with a TSA officer waiting to take tickets and identification, I break out in a sweat. I know that once I get there, I will hand them a card that holds my identity on it, a card that is a reminder that we are still here. More often than not, I will feel invalidated when I leave that desk, because even though airports are trained to receive our IDs, they don't understand what they are for, and so every encounter is a lesson in Indigenous history and evidence that we are still here.

As of 2018, there were 573 federally recognized Native tribes in the US. This means that many more tribes are not federally recognized, and those who are not enrolled with a tribe cannot use an identification card. As someone who is a citizen of a tribal nation, it is my responsibility to remind the world that we are still here but also to practice belonging whether I am a "citizen" or not, because kinship and belonging matter. Because we are erased in so many ways every single day, we must show that we still exist in any way we can.

"Our nations today are the embodiment of the fierce, desperate hope and relentless insistence of our ancestors to continue on in whatever way they could. Indigenous people today honour that determination by *being*."[1] Daniel Heath Justice points to the very reason I travel and let my identity be known. As a white-coded Potawatomi woman, I could make it easier on myself and the people around me by using my state-issued driver's license and getting through the line as quickly as possible. But knowing who I am and making that known is a tiny act of resistance, a way of honoring those who came before me and fought for our very existence. It is that embodiment of fierce, desperate hope that keeps me going every day, and the non-Native people in the airport security line should see that hope embodied. Other

Indigenous people who use their IDs when they travel sometimes share their stories online so that others can be aware of
our experiences; for Black and Brown Indigenous people, these
situations can feel traumatic, and non-Natives need to be aware
of that and show support.

One of the first times I traveled with my ID, the woman at the
desk demanded to see my driver's license anyway, and I obliged.
But the longer I travel, the more I realize how important it is to
stand up in these spaces, even if it causes a confrontation. The
second time I was asked, I stood my ground, reminding them that
in their own handbooks this is an acceptable form of ID. Native
people shouldn't have to be the ones doing this work. Once, a
woman named Officer Scott admitted how little she knew or was
trained to know about tribal IDs and assured me that she was
going to do better, learn more, and make it a priority. The best
experience was a woman who looked at my ID and said, "Why
would I look for an expiration date? You are forever." Every time I
use my tribal ID, it is an act of resistance. Every time I use it, it is
the work of educating people. Every time I use it, I am proclaiming that we are not invisible but are people who live full lives and
travel around the country and want to be recognized for who
we are.

Jean Dennison writes in her book, *Colonial Entanglement*,
about experiences of the Osage Nation in the US. When sharing about the importance and struggle of sovereignty, she says,
"American Indian nations have often run into direct conflict with
state and local governments as they have increasingly asserted
their sovereignty over their territories."[2]

The question is this: Who does our validation come from?
Does it come from the church, from American institutions, from
political spaces, from academia, or from our communities? Sovereignty is giving us the power to decide for ourselves as Indigenous
people who we will be, how we will live in community, and how
we will identify ourselves in the face of a settler colonial society.

Perhaps human nature has always been to take from, dominate, and erase others. Perhaps that is something we cannot escape. Over the last few years, we have become increasingly aware of the way Western Christianity erases the identity of others and centers itself again and again. This consistently puts white Christianity at the center of everything, calling whatever is outside it "other," "heathen," or "savage." I grew up in church spaces that constantly cast Christians as the light of the world while creating images of constant dark and hopelessness around the world outside the white, American church. When this happens, everywhere "out there" becomes a mission field. When we carry around these attitudes, everything revolves around how we think we have the answers, how we are "in" and everybody else is "out." It leaves us feeling like we must protect and defend everything about Christianity, and so we amp up our ideas of evangelism and often end up dehumanizing others in the process. Vice President Mike Pence, speaking to the National Rifle Association in 2019, badly misused a New Testament Scripture: "Remember that when we fight for freedom, we do not fight alone—because where the Spirit of the Lord is, there's freedom."[3] Pence is defending the right to bear arms, the right to "keep America free," by centering a Christianity that only wants what is best for itself—a xenophobic, homophobic, white supremacist religion that excludes all outside its walls, praises violence, and punishes those already on the margins.

In 2019 a white supremacist carried out two mass shootings at mosques in Christchurch, New Zealand. He killed fifty-one people and injured forty-nine more—people who were worshiping God. Fifty-one people were killed because someone thought it was their duty to make other human beings invisible because their religion and identities weren't pure enough. The Christians I encountered on social media that week nervously attended

churches on Sunday, wondering what they'd hear from the pulpit. The church I attended decided that day to pray for their own
evangelism training groups, and I left the church angrier than
I've been in a long time. In choosing to center Christianity, the
church erased the real danger of white supremacy in the world
and in our own religion, and also erased the real grief our Muslim
relatives faced in that tragedy.

We have to be able to hold the tension between faith and
religion, both when it gets things right and when it gets things
wrong. The work of the church has to be one of de-centering,
of recognizing the sacredness of both the earth and human beings of other faiths and religions, or those who do not actively
practice a faith at all. Instead of seeing everyone else as "lost" and
"in need of salvation," perhaps Christians can begin to see these
interactions as a learning tool, as a chance to see the divine face
of Mystery reflected in a neighbor, a relative, a stranger, a tree,
a bird, or a river.

People like Vice President Pence are the ones who call on
America's foundations as a *Christian nation* while continually
partnering with the president to silence the original peoples of
this land and lauding the work of oil companies. Invisibility is a
constant reality for Native people, as we are pushed behind sports
mascots that make us all out to be savage warriors or people
who have died off and no longer exist. We become invisible to
the people who say they are honoring us by honoring a mascot
called "redskins," a mascot based on genocide and the act of scalp-
ing Indigenous peoples. So much of America has held up these
stereotypes, celebrating the pastime of sports instead of the real
lives of Native peoples in America. The church has celebrated
violence by allowing guns inside its sanctuaries. In the work of
de-centering, in the work of listening to the voices of others who
have been treated badly by the church itself, the church must decide what kind of future it has in relation to the world around it.
The church can either bear good fruit that brings an abundance

of inclusive goodness or bear rotten fruit that will corrupt the world with more pain, oppression, and violence in its wake.

PART 4 SUMMARY

Work, as it turns out, isn't always what we think it is. It is gift. It is writing letters and sitting in the sun watching a grasshopper. It is marching in a protest or protesting by drinking morning coffee and being present to one another. In a world of workaholics, work isn't just about getting things done but is its own kind of *being*, just as Original Man and the animals had to keep watch as the earth formed. Work is *keeping watch*, and keeping watch *is work*. Because what comes from that work is the fruit of a new thing, a new world, a new beginning. The asking, searching, finding, and working, it all leads us here, to a new way, to a better way, to a *softer way*. May we go.

Bearing Fruit in a New World

New land grew from what they planted on the turtle's back,
larger and larger so that eventually,
they could walk freely on the land again.
They called it Turtle Island.
They called it Home.

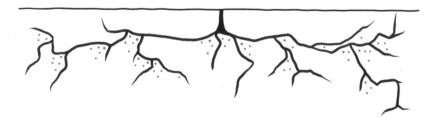

There is a path,
outside the doors
of the church halls
or the parish home.

There is a path
that leads to God.

There is a room,
a sanctuary of
limbs and boughs,
with a choir
of nightingales
in the oak loft.

There are pews,
carved by the bodies
of lone elms,
fallen, brown,
ready for you.

There is a sermon,
told in the wind
as she blows by

your face,
a sermon in
the heartbeat of the earth.

There is a path,
a path that leads to God.

Faces of stones and dirt,
old enough to tell us stories
about the long-ago Ones.

Those worshiping people
found sanctuary
and pew
and choir
and sermon
among the woodlands,
in the plains,
at the peak of a mountain,
next to the daisies
and wild waters.

They found the path,
and they knew God.

17

Finding One Another

Natasha Morrison began Be the Bridge in 2016 as a space for the church to foster conversations on racial reconciliation and justice. When our church in Atlanta announced that it was participating, I joined right away, because I was hungry for conversations on intersectionality and truth-telling, especially within a church context. Over the next few months, a group of about twelve of us met to share our stories, led by our group leader, Zach, who facilitated the conversations. The people of color in the room shared their experiences in America, and I shared my experiences as an Indigenous woman. We became close, not because we have a lot in common but because we gathered for the purpose of listening, of making room, of testing the status quo given to us for so long both in America and in the church.

Intersectionality as an idea was discussed as early as 1892 by Anna J. Cooper, a Black liberation activist and educator. The term *intersectionality* was coined more recently, in 1989, by Kimberlé Crenshaw, a pioneer of critical race theory, who gave a TED talk on the subject.[1] She defines intersectionality as "the complex, cumulative manner in which the effects of different forms of discrimination combine, overlap, or intersect." Crenshaw's work focuses on the intersection of race and gender, and on how race and gender overlap to disenfranchise Black women. She says, "We have to be willing to bear witness to the often painful realities that we would just rather not confront." What I see in these expressions is the invisibility of Indigenous women in America as well. I learned in my Be the Bridge group and from the Black women in my life that Black and Indigenous women must work together, must partner together, and must actively join with other women of color to lead the way forward in America. Intersectionality brings us together, because Black women, Indigenous women, and other women of color across the spectrum are ignored, mistreated, and called *angry* for speaking up about basic human rights. Bridging this gap means having more conversations on intersectionality within our churches and communities. It means men stepping down and women stepping up to tell our stories. Leanne Betasamosake Simpson says, "For me, engagement with the theories and practices of co-resistors is powerful because it often illuminates colonial thinking in myself, and demonstrates different possibilities in analysis and action in response to similar systems of oppression and dispossession."[2]

At the 2019 Oscars, in his acceptance speech for the award won by his film *BlacKkKlansman*, Spike Lee called on Black and Indigenous peoples to honor our ancestors by working together, by rising together in America in 2019 and 2020 as the presidential election draws closer. It was a beautiful message of solidarity that we all need to hold on to as we do this difficult work. I am reminded of my friend Darryl, a Black pastor in Atlanta, and of my good friend Amena, an incredible poet and writer. We meet for coffee every now and then to discuss the ways in which our identities overlap and differ, and these conversations bring us solidarity. They help us remain willing to do the work necessary to make justice happen, especially within the church.

Intersectionality also stretches into interspiritual dialogue, spaces in which, as an Indigenous woman and a Christian, I listen to my Muslim, Sikh, Buddhist, Hindu, atheist, and Jewish friends. Just as the religious rights of Indigenous peoples have been taken away in America throughout history, the religious rights of many minority cultures and religions have been taken, and we need to have these conversations about revival, renewal, and, in some cases, reparations. In the era of Trump, when hate crimes are high, we need to listen to these voices. In 2017, hate crimes rose 17 percent, and a large number of those hate crimes were anti-Semitic.[3] My friend Arjun Singh Sethi, a Sikh lawyer, activist, and educator, released a book in 2018 called *American Hate: Survivors Speak Out* in which he chronicles stories of hate crimes across many races, religions, and ethnic groups. He says in the introduction, "The rhetoric and policies of this administration, and the hate and bigotry of everyday people, have terrorized communities in ways that we still cannot fully comprehend."[4] I met Arjun in 2018 at an event in Atlanta while he was on his book tour. This is what the work of solidarity is: at an event to celebrate his own book, Arjun invited people that he knew and trusted to share about *their* work so that together, we might all fight against hate. It is essential that in America today, we stand with one another, we practice solidarity with one another, and we work to dismantle any institutions that have oppressed people throughout time, even if it is, indeed, the church.

In America, Black people, Indigenous people, other people of color, and religious minorities have run out of time. There is no more time to tiptoe around conversations, no more time for white people to say, "This isn't who we are!" There is no more time for Indigenous bodies, women's bodies, two-spirit Indigenous bodies, trans bodies, Sikh bodies, Asian bodies, disabled bodies, or Black bodies to be attacked and for everyone to misunderstand why it happened. *This is the America we know and have always known.* History tells the story, and if we can't gather in a living room to tell the truth and listen to one another, we will never gather in the streets, in our churches, or in our political spaces to ask for change. It must begin with our experiences, with our words, and with our bodies, and lead us to a better way forward.

In the summer of 2018, Travis and I celebrated our ten-year anniversary. We'd had an intense season over the last few years; he'd been in a PhD program in political science at a nearby university, and I'd just published my first book, *Glory Happening: Finding the Divine in Everyday Places*. We were tired, a little traumatized, and working to create space for each other and fruitful conversations as we dreamed of the future. In the midst of that, we were remembering and celebrating the ten years we'd been married. So we decided to get tattoos, and as the day approached, I struggled with what to get.

We booked an appointment for our tattoos, celebrating who we were when we were first married and who we are today, people who are the same but different, people who have grown but are still growing.

I was scrolling through Instagram posts when I came across a picture by Chief Lady Bird, a Chippewa/Potawatomi artist in Canada. The artwork on the post represented the seven generations, seven flowers reaching up toward a bright yellow sun, back to our ancestors, back to the beginning before colonization took so much from us. Our Seven Fires/Seven Generations story tells the journey of our people, our struggles and triumphs, our interactions with whiteness, and our hope that future generations will choose to remember what it means to be Potawatomi so that our culture will not only survive but thrive. The seventh generation is the time when the young people will return to our ways, seeking to know what it means to be Potawatomi, to be Anishinaabe. This story means so much to my journey, and it keeps me tethered to who I am so that I can remind my two children who they are as we journey together.

So, with permission, I got the image designed by Chief Lady Bird on my left inside forearm. The process was akin to giving birth to my babies without pain medication to numb labor; I practiced deep breaths every time the needle dug into my skin, a process that I knew would bring to life something new on my body and inside my soul.

In the following weeks as I tended to this fresh wound on my skin, I thought about what it means to heal. I thought about the Indigenous friends I've been finding along the way in this journey. I thought about the incredible work they do, people like Chief Lady Bird. I thought about how our individual healing is tied to our universal healing and how breaking the bonds of colonization is an essential part of that. As the flakes of skin peeled off to reveal the finished image, the realization cemented itself in me: I belong to my ancestors, I belong to those who came before, to a vision of all of us that keeps us tethered. The work that we must do together, whether we all get tattoos or not, is to help each other see that vision of wholeness beyond colonization and hate. We must carry one another's stories with grace and honor, and lead each other toward a kind of healing that heals whole systems, not just people. If we have learned anything from the church, and if we have learned anything from injustice, we know that it is individuals who act as a part of systems that continue oppressive cycles, yet those same individuals can band together to create change. When we call out racism, yes, we are calling out our own hearts, but we are calling out the systems that have created that hate, and the decisions we make as a whole within our institutions that propel us toward hate and ignorance instead of toward truth-telling wholeness. But if we choose to really *see* one another, we will work toward healing, and it will look like the seventh generation finding their way home again.

I started therapy for the first time in my life when I was thirty years old. I found a trauma counselor who deals with intersectionality, and as a mixed Indigenous woman, I was hopeful that she'd help me work through some difficult parts of my life. What I wasn't expecting was how she helps me tell my own story. She is helping me see that transformation is part of healing, and that healing cannot happen unless we honestly ask how we came to be. We cannot heal until we discover the wound, and naming our trauma is part of that process. Finally, I began to understand that trauma is real and has consequences, including the trauma and consequences of years of cultural genocide and forced assimilation of Indigenous peoples that I carry inside my bones. Giving a name and a face to every real trauma in my life allows me to ask what it means to heal from it. And beyond that, I discover that in decolonizing, I am healing every single day.

This is where community comes in. This is where the hard work of brushing up against the stories of others comes to meet us, comes to ask us difficult questions of ourselves. If we hold grace for our own story, we can reach across dividing lines to say, "I see *your* story. I see *your* experiences. They matter. Let's *decolonize* together."

The story of my dear friend, an immigrant from Ethiopia, matters. The story of every missing and murdered Indigenous woman matters. The stories of resilience and hope among people of color and disabled people matters, just as the stories of LGBTQ+ youth who have been turned out of their homes and the church matter.

With so many conversations about white supremacy, hate, racism, and toxic patriarchy, we aren't going to get anywhere unless we consider *narrative*. We've got to honestly talk about the story America is telling itself and the truth of where we came from: we were built by settler colonialism, by one group (and later many more groups) pushing out another group to create a culture that identifies itself by toxic empire. If we start there, with that recognition, we will move forward, just as I moved forward in my own process of healing. When we name our trauma, when we name the parts of our story that have been in hiding, we come closer to naming truth.

And when we name truth, we call our fear into the light. We face it.

"I think of a good conversation as an adventure," Krista Tippett said.[5] If conversation is an adventure, so too are the stories we tell within those conversations, the glimpses we get into the lives and experiences of others. Maybe we are all just barely getting started. Maybe we are all transforming, whether we know it or not, and we are simply to hold on and wait to see what's on the other side.

In the Ojibwe creation story, when Original Man and the wolf walk the earth, they spend time with one another and with all of creation. They tell each other *stories*. They build community, and when the time comes, Great Spirit separates them so they can go on their own journeys, always repeating those stories they shared together.

What we learn from Original Man and the wolf is that our time is limited. While we are here, we invest in our own stories, our own healing, and in the stories and healing of others.

We walk the earth and learn what it means to be communal.

We honor the work of transformation, recognizing that we can't possibly truly transform unless we are actively decolonizing along the way.

18

The Future of Decolonization

OUR SPIRITUAL REALITIES do not exist in a vacuum. To be connected to our own spirituality, we must be connected to the spirituality of others. This means our spirituality is directly tied to institutions that police the spiritual lives of others. The fact that Indigenous ceremonies were banned in the US until 1978 and continue to be restricted is proof. In 1978, the American Indian Religious Freedom Act was passed by President Jimmy Carter so that Indigenous peoples would have protections for religious ceremonies in the US, a right that has often not been protected but instead has been violated by the government.

We have always been here, but what does it do to our spiritual essence to know that we will be punished for expressing our ways of knowing Creator, and how does that actually affect our connectedness as a whole? Colonization and white supremacy steal so much from Indigenous peoples and from Black peoples who were stolen from their homelands and enslaved in the US, and we cannot deny that this history is a spiritual one. So today, my spiritual liberation is tied up with the spiritual liberation of all my relatives who face oppression, whose bodies are policed and told that they are less than—are we not working to be liberated together, and are our spirits not bound together to fight institutional injustices that have existed in America since its beginning? Everyone who joins in this space with us is joining the work of fighting systems of dehumanization, and is joining in the lifelong work of decolonizing. We are bearing good fruit in hopes of creating newness in the world.

Telling women that we do not matter as much as men do is dehumanizing and damaging to the soul. The way that Christianity has appropriated and erased Jewish history and culture and practiced anti-Semitism is dehumanizing. So, decolonization is a spiritual matter just as it is a physical, mental, social, and political one. We have to see it in a holistic light.

The day I went to Lake Michigan, the original home of my people, for the first time, it was a perfect, windy spring morning in April. My dear friend Amy drove us in her minivan, forty minutes away from the city to a small town with tall trees that was now inhabited by people of Dutch heritage. We drove up to an area with a playground and picnic tables, and we climbed a set of stairs to reach the water.

Growing up around tiny lakes in the Midwest, my imagination did not lend itself to what Lake Michigan might actually be. So, when we took that last step of the uphill climb to look out at the beach before us, my breath caught in my chest.

White sand.

Waves.

Deadwood.

Teenagers huddled under towels and blankets.

Wind.

Memories.

I took off my shoes and walked as fast as I could, Amy trailing behind me with her camera. She said she'd capture this moment for me. The photos would keep me tethered to this place for years to come, the photos would help me remember. The quiet presence of the water lapped in and out with every wave, and I watched. I listened.

I whispered, *Migwetch, Mamogosnan, Migwetch, Migwetch,* over and over again, a prayer of gratitude for that moment that held me. And while I prayed, while I laid tobacco over the water's crisp, iridescent skin, I was told to remember. The water told me to remember what I may not even consciously know.

The water has supplied life to us and nurtured us. We are simply recipients of gift upon gift.

I was asked to imagine the before—before those stairs were built to bring us to the shore, before there were paved parking lots and playgrounds. When it was just the people and the land, there was no room for colonizer thinking or actions.

When it was just the people and the land, we built fires and grew wild rice.

When it was just the people and the land, white supremacy was never an option.

We stayed there for about an hour, collecting pebbles and shells to take home to my children, and a piece of driftwood that sits in my home today and tells my own story back to me.

I was in Michigan for a conference, but before it started, I wanted to see the water, the water that my people once knew, the water that the Potawatomi people still know. Those that knew the significance of being in Michigan approached me throughout the weekend asking quietly, "So, how has it been for you to be here?" I'd smile and give a summary answer, "It's been so great," but I didn't really have words for the weight, the gravity of it all.

I felt like a stranger to a land that knew me. I felt like the prodigal son returning to a father with open arms, only the thing that took me away was the gunpoint of forced removal.

The land and the water tell stories we cannot conceive of, even when we listen. And so, we just trust. We watch the water and let it give whatever it needs to give, and we receive it with open arms. This is the way.

It's difficult to imagine our cities as something other than what they are. It's difficult to think of them without buildings, streets, or storefronts. But if we can remember that they were once lands inhabited by Indigenous peoples, many cultures who stood on this ground and acknowledged the sacredness of the hills, mountains, and waters, many people *who still do*, maybe we can remember that this land is *still* sacred, that it is *still* space that we should inhabit while honoring it and the people who care for it.

This is what Lake Michigan is.

For the world to survive, for true justice to take place among us, decolonization must be a goal. We must fight against systems of colonial settler oppression—systems like toxic patriarchy and capitalist greed that give no care to the land—and we must do it together for the sake of all of us, telling our stories in those spaces. Carolina Hinojosa-Cisneros, a prophetic Tejana poet, says in a piece she wrote for *On Being* that storytelling is a lifeline in her family and the fuel that continues to lead her to decolonization. "In the nook of my grandfather's arm, I learned of Moses and how he freed the Israelites. I wept as my grandfather recounted working in the cotton fields under the laborious sun that nearly turned his body into a leather purse."[1]

Carolina reminds us that prayer is poetry, that poetry is storytelling, and that even our painful stories lead us out of the bondage of white supremacy and into liberation for ourselves and those around us.

Decolonization is not just for the oppressed. It is a gift for everyone. Just as growing pains hurt before the actual growth takes place, so it hurts to decolonize. For some, it hurts like hell, and then one day, we all appear on the other side of it, healed, our stories told in all their truth. Just like that, we all gather to bathe in the healing waters, and just like that, everyone is made clean.

In the winter of 2019, the Indigenous Peoples March in Washington, DC, was interrupted when a confrontation broke out. Nathan Phillips, an elder of the Omaha tribe, began to sing a famous song from the American Indian Movement as he stepped in between a group of Black Israeli protestors and white high schoolers from Covington Catholic, a private school in Kentucky. As Phillips sang and the confrontation between the two groups subsided, the young boys began to taunt him, one standing in his face as he sang and played his drum. Some did the tomahawk chop, a famous action from Atlanta Braves games, while others yelled, "Build the wall!" The media caught on to the story, spinning it in all sorts of directions, many of them centering the voices of the young Catholic boys in the confrontation. Some news outlets reached out to Indigenous writers to cover the story, but despite sharing our words and experiences, we watched the white story get centered over the Indigenous story once again, and those of us who have connected the dots throughout history know that this is not a one-time thing. One of the boys from the confrontation, Nick Sandmann, later tried to sue CNN in a defamation suit.

History has tried again and again to silence Indigenous voices. We are pushed to the side, criminalized, or covered up. The *New York Post* published an article listing the "criminal record" of Phillips, putting his past mistakes on display in order to taint his reputation.[2] This is a common theme throughout Indigenous history in the US, a theme that our ancestors faced and that we continue to face. The taunting faces of white oppression continue generation to generation, in small and large ways. They continue in the harassment of Indigenous children; they continue in forced assimilation and in accounts of toxic stereotyping. Our ancestors, in all that they had to endure, prepared us for this moment in time. They prepared us for an America in which Donald Trump could be president and discrimination could run freely across our computer screens, without anyone noticing how it affects

Indigenous peoples. So, as always, it is the responsibility of those of us who are alive today to decide what kind of ancestors we will be to those who come after us.

Will we be the ones who stand up against injustice, or will we be the ones who leave them with raging fires and messes to clean up once we are gone? This is how we get narratives about Columbus as a kind explorer or about the Pilgrims who arrived and cooperated right away with those they encountered. It's how we have generations of adults who don't know that there are currently 573 federally recognized Native tribes in the US.

When whiteness runs the narrative, we have to ask how and why.

Why aren't stories of Indigenous resistance taught in schools? Why aren't our cultures celebrated for what they contribute, even to modern-day society? Because the Indigenous story has been buried under the white story, it will take a lot of work to uncover it. It will take more than Indigenous peoples to do the work—it will take *all* people. Decolonization doesn't mean we go back to the beginning, but it means we fix what is broken now, for future generations. If you're a teacher, it means you read books by Indigenous authors and you teach differently. If you're a church leader, it means you change the narrative about reaching Indigenous nations and other forms of missions and recognize that, often, evangelism is erasure, and a listening relationship is something altogether different. If you're a professor, it means bringing resources to your students that will challenge them to look outside the white narrative. If you're a business owner, it means you work to diversify the workplace and root out toxic masculinity. If you're an activist, take to social media and begin listening and following Indigenous people, and let that influence your everyday life. If you're a parent, introduce your children to the idea that Indigenous peoples are still *alive*, still *thriving*, still creating and contributing to the good things that happen in the world.

If we cannot begin where we are, we will have a hard time changing anything outside of us. Decolonization is always an invitation.

I am involved in many circles of people, especially on Twitter and Facebook, who are having conversations not just about deconstruction but about reconstruction as well. Reconstruction is asking how we rebuild community and life now that we're adults, now that we are trying to make sense of the ways we may have grown up in toxic religious environments.

It's a strange time we live in, because we have face-to-face community, but we also have this community we build with people all over the country, all over the world. The power of social media gives us an opportunity to be tethered to one another in a different way. It exposes us to those who are different than we are and gives us a chance to live as communal people. But often, deconstruction within the church ends up being very individualistic.

What does it look like to deconstruct and reconstruct as a *people*, as *kin*, to take on the work of creating a postcolonial church for the sake of all of us, for the sake of the oppressed, for the sake of the earth? Is it possible?

As Americans? As Christians?

We have this split between what it means to live communally, to practice our faith—the work of justice—on an institutional level and what it means to practice justice on an individual level. I think both are necessary, but if we cannot remember that we do the individual work because we are connected to each other, we're going to miss out on everything. We will not work against systems that oppress.

In fact, we may, quite possibly, continue the work of colonization and oppression without realizing it.

Donald Trump, in a speech to the Naval Academy, said, "Our ancestors tamed a continent!"[3] If a colonizing sentence ever existed, it's this one, spoken by a president. In response, Indigenous peoples reminded him that we are not to be tamed. Our Potawatomi ancestors, who lived full lives in the Great Lakes region before being forcefully removed at gunpoint to Kansas, knew what it meant to live, and once they arrived in Kansas and later in Oklahoma, they continued to adapt, continued to find a way as America was building itself off of their oppression and the oppression of others like them. Our ancestors lived off the land. They asked permission to take what they needed from her. They prayed with tobacco, a gift given to us by Creator, as medicine and as a tool for prayer. They walked with Mystery, telling creation stories. But to the white, Euro-Christian psyche, this was not acceptable. Being "untamed" meant being uncivilized, and being uncivilized is just bad for business—the business of mixing God with empire. And so, after years of genocide, forced assimilation, Indian boarding schools, forced land removal, displacement, massacres, and history books covering up all of it, here I am, a woman who is a citizen of the Potawatomi nation, a woman of European descent, asking what it means to be who I am today. And there are so many others like me.

For so long, the only *right way* has been the *American way*, and the American way was always to assimilate into culture, to stop learning our language, to stop telling our stories, to fit in, to look as white as possible. It's what my ancestors ended up doing in Oklahoma, and it's why I grew up knowing nothing about Potawatomi culture but everything about Southern Baptist culture and about a white missionary Jesus. It's why I grew up not knowing how to pray traditionally or how to speak our Potawatomi language.

What does it mean to be Indigenous and to have ties to the person of Jesus without being tied to the destructive, colonizing institution of the church? It is a constant decolonizing. It is a constant longing for interaction with others who, following the Universal Christ, as Richard Rohr calls it, can take on the hope of a decolonizing faith. It is sharing space with Black people, Indigenous people, and other people of color, and letting our experiences shape each other. It means interacting with my white friends, having really difficult conversations, and facing my own privilege in that conversation as well. Deconstruction and decolonization can be partners, along with grief and truth-telling. May we learn from this community that we are called to the bigger work ahead of us, so that, together, we know what it means to return to Mystery that has always wanted *all of us*. May we do this work together so that, each day that we move on, we are building a future that is made for everyone.

19

Returning

Everything comes from something that came before,
which was once nothing.

Tommy Orange, *There, There*

ABOUT TWO YEARS after my first trip to Sweetwater Creek, we returned to the water. I stood watching the water rush over the rocks, and I was ushered back again, asked to look and remember. We spend our whole lives asking ourselves who we are and what we should be about, but what if those things are the forces that find us, some sort of sacred movement on the wind that does not let us go but tarries here and there, letting us know of its presence?

For over twenty years of my life I spent little time knowing or asking to be known by this Mystery, this sacred space of who I am and will always be. Now that I've found her, I cannot let her go. She is my essence, the voice that calls me back to myself, to the land, to the people, to *Kche Mnedo*, the one who leads.

It is no coincidence that Sweetwater Creek on Muscogee Creek and Cherokee land found me, that an evening spent walking a short trail led me straight to myself. So I walk it, and on this visit, I ask the waters what they speak of, what they've seen in their long and wise years.

And I ask the cicadas in the trees who their ancestors used to sing to, ask those trees what kind of creatures have climbed them and napped in their shade—and the reality is that it was all sorts: the Cherokee people and the ants, enslaved people and plantation owners, mill workers, squirrels, soldiers, tired fathers, mothers, and children.

The water told me to keep my eyes open. We are told to pay attention.

What does it look like to return, again and again, to the voice of Mystery in our lives? Perhaps it looks like building relationships with people who are not like us. Perhaps it requires following people on social media who come from different racial or religious backgrounds. Perhaps it means letting the earth speak and taking the time to listen. It always means asking how we can become people who love better.

One of my favorite church seasons is Lent, the forty days before Easter in which we remember that we come from dust, and we will return to it. The Potawatomi word for earth is *aki*, and it speaks to this same idea—we are made from earth, from dirt. This is a universal belief and does not just belong to the church, and yet, growing up I had never heard of Lent. As an adult, I've learned that it's a time in which the church is brought into a space of wilderness to ask who we are and where we are headed. When you live on the outside, you know the liminal spaces, the in-between spaces, the *thin places* where you feel the physical and spiritual intertwine. I believe that's what Jesus's life was marked by. As Richard Rohr writes, "People who empty themselves in the wilderness always meet a God who is greater than they would have dared to hope."[1]

It is what Indigenous peoples find when we fast, pray, listen, engage.

It is what people who long for sacredness find when they take the time to listen.

So, for Lent in 2019, I decided to spend more intentional time outside.

I went into our backyard and touched the trees.

I gazed out windows more often.

I sat still because I knew I should.

I remembered in that space my *dust-to-dustness* once again, and there I remembered what it means to pray.

We pray because the creatures of the earth teach us how to pray.

We lament because creation laments, and we must work to fix what we've broken.

We repair because God is always repairing.

And we decolonize because it is always a return to the kindness of Mystery.

It is also a return to asking hard questions, to making room for the work of forging a new path. Rachel Held Evans wrote, "The prophet's voice is routinely dismissed as too critical, but she always challenges from a place of deep love for her community."[2] She is commenting on that important piece of stepping into the church or whatever community we are part of. When we step into it, we make room for change, and the wisdom to bring that change is often born in the wilderness, in darkness, even in grief. We bring up hard things like history, and we challenge ourselves to make things better for future generations. It must be the only way.

The earth leads us. The water leads us. And to bear fruit for a better world, we must lead one another.

Living in Atlanta as a Potawatomi woman has been challenging. Here, history of who originally inhabited this land, the

Muscogee Creek and Cherokee peoples, is covered up by other history. It's covered up by Confederate history, and it seems that in many spaces, it's difficult for people to draw connections from the forced removal of the Indigenous peoples of this land to the mistreatment and enslavement of African peoples when they were taken from their homes and forced here on ships. Atlanta is a transient city, with people moving in and out every few years for work and school. One day, I found a group of Indigenous people who gather in my city. As we got to know each other, I knew what it felt like to be home, even though I'm miles from my own tribe, hometown, and family.

Like on the day I returned to Sweetwater Creek, I returned to parts of myself that had long been ignored. My friend Meredith and I would get coffee every now and then, and I noticed the magic that happens between two Indigenous women who share space together. We laughed. We talked about traumatic things that only Indigenous women can explain with tears in our eyes. We celebrated the work of Indigenous peoples all around us. And then we laughed more. You see, when Indigenous peoples come together to share our stories and our cultures, we are joining our ancestors throughout time who banded together to fight assimilation, oppression, and genocide, who laughed together because it was medicine. We remember them when we look in each other's eyes.

One day the group of us met at a coffee shop, and Melanie and Meredith brought their beading. My oldest son, Eliot, was with me. He watched these two women work, one on earrings, another on designs for a skirt. He watched in awe, connecting dots in his own head. Melanie handed him some beads, thread, and a needle, and he began his own little project. I watched in awe as my son began to heal some of my own scars, as he began to renew something in me. He has a chance to know what it means to be Potawatomi far more than I ever did, and I plan to give him that chance. My youngest son, Isaiah, has been tasked by his father to *find things that are wrong and make them right*, and I can see those thoughts taking shape in him, even as a five-year-old. I can see him thinking on a communal level, wondering at things like the legacy of Martin Luther King Jr., who was assassinated, who was targeted by a government and a white church that did not want freedom from white supremacy. My son is wondering about the Thanksgiving story we tell, about what it means to speak the truth when it matters.

Both my sons will learn these stories and know why they are important because they have been to places like Sweetwater Creek, and they know the power that water holds. They know the power that Indigenous women hold, and they know the power that they themselves hold in one day being men who will carry on a legacy of fighting injustice and oppression, a legacy that always calls them home.

❧

The story of the prodigal son, one I've mentioned a few times in this book, is told again and again in the church as a triumphant story about a son who went astray, who degraded his father's name, returning home to his father's open arms and a celebration in his honor. Many Christians like to use this story to talk about those who have wandered away from the church, the ones they believe are on the outside and trying to get right with God again, the ones God welcomes back with open arms.

I don't know what it means to waste a life, if that is even possible, and I don't know that we can step so far outside the love of Mystery that we are not seen and known even in that distance. But there is always something important about *returning*. There is always something about the way a community welcomes us home. Young people who are forced out of their communities by traumatic events must return home and learn what it means to be part of their people again. I think about young Black men who are wrongfully imprisoned in the United States, who return home to reintegrate into society. I think about LGBTQ+ youth who are kicked out of their homes and communities and must find new homes with strangers who welcome them in. I think of Indigenous people separated from their communities through boarding schools, who must learn what it means to know themselves when their stories are riddled with trauma.

The work of returning is communal work, and we must all lead one another. When I sit down to write and tell my own story, I can feel the fire burn brighter again, and the work of returning leads me deeper into who I am and who God is.

I come again to the reality of myself, of my name, of my people. I remember, I tell the stories, I let my experiences flow from my fingers into a machine that cannot possibly process them but can record them for the future, for my children, for those who will never know my life experiences. I let the stories flow from my mouth so that they are embedded into the bodies of my own children, who will carry them forward. The fire must be lit and the fire must be re-lit, for all of us to remember, to know, to find the way home.

So many of us have forgotten the way home, the way back to ourselves, so we must support one another on the journey; it may begin with setting healthy habits for ourselves, but it will lead to healing all around us. Buy books from women of color. Support Indigenous artists. Give your money to organizations that are working to break down toxic systems like patriarchy, sexism, ableism, and homophobia. The only way we can make our way home is to support one another on the journey.

When I arrived to speak at the 2018 Evolving Faith conference, Sarah Bessey and Rachel Held Evans took the time to tell me that they appreciated my presence, and they gave me a card and a gift so I would know that they saw the weight I carry when I speak in predominantly white, non-Native spaces. They were letting me know that on my journey toward finding myself and finding my way home, they would stand beside me in the questions and the difficulties, and they would see that the work Indigenous people, Black people, and other people of color do costs us a lot. It costs us a lot of energy, because the work of returning to ourselves, the work of fighting against systems of whiteness, is traumatic. If we are free to be ourselves in those traumatic spaces, to have people we can trust, who will truly hold space with us, we will all learn to find our way home, wherever home may be. Sometimes home is land, like it is land to Indigenous peoples. But home is also a space inside ourselves and with others that we can return to, a space we can find that we've never been to before, where we are accepted as we are with all the implications that has for the church, for America, for our systems, for the world. If we can return to the essence of our identities, we can teach the children around us to know who they are from a young age, and perhaps one day, when they are older, when they create the future, they will work together to change things and to heal systems we had no idea how to heal.

20

A New World for Our Children

> We Ojibwe tend to be sentimental about our children,
> who are the heart and future of the people. Greatly loved
> as they are, their existence has such importance to not only
> their families but all Anishinaabeg that they will not know
> until they are adults themselves just how much they mean
> to us and the many reasons why.
>
> Linda LeGarde Grover, *Onigamiising*

MY OLDEST SON, ELIOT, once told me that his favorite stories of the Hebrew Bible and New Testament are Moses parting the Red Sea to liberate his people from slavery and Jesus using his spit and dirt to make mud so he could heal a man of blindness. Whether he realizes it or not, Eliot is tied up in stories of liberation. He is wired for seeking justice and creating a world in which that justice becomes a reality. That is the power of storytelling.

I believe that all children are liberators, and we must remember what power they hold as our future. They marvel at the stories of prophets. They long to make things right. They see the face of God, *Mamogosnan*, Mystery, *Kche Mnedo, Yahweh*. They see the power women hold, before we taint them with toxic patriarchy and lies about what it means to be masculine. Our young women will lead us, and our young men will walk with respect and kindness, but sometimes, we must get out of the way. During the week of Martin Luther King Jr.'s birthday in 2019, my youngest son, Isaiah Desmond (named after both the prophet Isaiah and the prophet Desmond Tutu), learned about King's legacy in his kindergarten class. On drives to and from school we talked about King, and I reminded Isaiah of the importance of speaking the truth. Eliot and Isaiah's school is the same school that wrongfully taught about the Pilgrims and Indians living in harmony during Thanksgiving, and yet here we were, my five-year-old son telling me that King died at the hands of another man, that he was assassinated for speaking the truth. We must tell our children the *whole* truth, and we must begin today, or we will repeat the same lies taught in our schools, often taught in our churches and by our government, again and again.

In our Potawatomi teachings, we believe we are in the time of the seventh fire, the seventh prophecy, when the young people will return to our ways, take up our traditions, learn our language, and put things right again. It must be the young people, because they are our future. I did not grow up knowing my tribe's history. I did not grow up knowing that we had our own language or our own stories. I grew up celebrating the daring work of Columbus, just like every other child around me. Now that I am a mother, I want to give my children a better story, so that when they come up against injustice, they know the truth. I want them to have the truth embedded in their own stories so that when they come across injustice toward others, they can connect the dots and see that oppression comes in many forms, that the oppressed must stand up for one another, and that we must use our privilege in its varying layers to make change when and where we can. I want them to understand who they come from and that their identity carries privilege, privilege that they must use for good.

Empowering our children, whether they are our children biologically or children in our community, means letting the stories of the oppressed reach them, and if they are descendants of the oppressed, letting their bodies and souls sink into their own reality, so that they become the fire that burns bright for future generations. It means that sometimes we need to let our children see our anger, and we need to let them see us channel that anger into good that transforms something, someone, somewhere.

Lately, at the dinner table and then again at bedtime, my kids ask us to tell them stories from our childhood. We don't tell them just the great ones, because, at the end of the day, our children don't need to see us tallying off all the ways we've behaved or been blessed throughout our life. They need to see that we are *human*. They need to hear our stories of grief and pain, our stories of celebration and our stories of loss. We need to name some of our mistakes for them. We need to tell the truth about the systems that we work with and against. Our children will take those stories with them, and they will remember that it is important to listen to the land. They will remember that it is important to pay attention to mistakes and listen to their own souls. They will remember our stories, and our stories will shape them. Our own vulnerability with the truth will teach them to be vulnerable with the truth, and with that, they will lead us all.

❧—✿—❧

One afternoon as we were getting ready to move from one house to another across town, I was going through old containers of our belongings. The week before, my therapist asked me if I had any journals from when I was young, and I found them, beginning in fourth grade, right after my parents divorced. I found journals with notes on every sin I believed I'd committed, every shame that hung over my head. I told God I was sorry more than I reminded myself that I am loved and valuable and sacred. The church taught me to view my life as a series of boxes to be ticked off, every day a choice: Did you save someone's soul from hell, or didn't you? Did you sin, or didn't you? Were you pure, or weren't you?

And yet, I hope something different for my children. I hope something for their future that begins with the sacredness of who they are, that begins with the sacredness of this earth and the many gifts she pours over us day after day. Richard Rohr writes, "We'll never solve the way to a new life in our heads; we have to live our way into a new kind of thinking."[1] This is exactly what the children around us embody for us. If my children can remember that the things they experience, including all the people and creatures around them, are sacred, maybe they won't grow up commodifying everything and everyone. Maybe they will learn what it means to live a constantly decolonizing existence, to value what is often forgotten around us, to love people and our creature kin simply because they were created to be loved.

In 2019 one of our dear friends who is Jewish invited us to his home for a Seder dinner to commemorate Passover. This same friend has brought us into his home many times, sharing his culture with us, letting us sit in his presence and see a reality that is different from ours but that teaches us the most powerful lessons on resilience and love. That night, as my two boys sat at both ends of the table listening intently, our friend Daniel walked us through the story of the Hebrew people—slavery, liberation, and joining in the work of freedom with their friends, including Indigenous people. My children will always remember dipping parsley into salt water to remind them of the bitterness of hate and slavery, and they will always remember singing and eating with the adults in the room as we talked about what freedom might look like for all people. In the church, instead of learning to fight against injustice, particularly for Jewish people, we were taught anti-Semitic messages, such as the notion that Jews were to blame for Jesus's death. My boys will come alongside their Jewish kin, and also their friends of other religions and cultures, to fight against injustice, just as they join with their Christian friends to create a better, more loving world. Our children must learn that to become a more complete representation of God in the world, we must learn to see the sacred value of God in one another.

This is what I hope for my children, for your children, for my neighbors next door, for the people across the ocean that I will never meet. If we can learn to believe not just that people are sacred but also that the earth is sacred, that she is our teacher, that the creatures around us are sacred, maybe our children will be able to pave the way for a better future for all of us. Maybe they will be the ones who fight climate change, who save our rainforests, who write in their journals, "I know I am beloved, I know this earth is beloved, I know my neighbor is beloved."

We live in an era in which the young people are leading us. They are leading us on issues of gun control; they are leading us on issues of climate change; they are leading protests and marches and making phone calls to their senators. They are changing systems that must be changed. Some of them are showing up to vote because they know that they are the holders of the future. They know that they have a chance to change things, and we should give them everything they need to do it. Being a parent means participating in the active, communal work of loving and letting go of our children, of preparing and sending out to make room on the earth for more love and hope. That stretches beyond religion, beyond culture, beyond family name. It is the work of the human soul.

And it is also beyond the work of parenthood. All of our children belong to all of us, because that's what kinship does. It's a reminder of that dust we came from and of that dust we will return to. It's a reminder that while we are here, we make room for the next generation to spring up from the soil and create a new landscape. So our Native children lead us. Our children of color lead us. Our daughters lead us. Our queer and gender nonbinary children lead us. Our disabled children lead us. The ones that are forgotten lead us. The ones that are told to be quiet at the dinner table lead us, and if we are smart, we will let them lead. And if we are smart, we will see that we all return to Mystery, to *Kche Mnedo*, and we are simply to learn what we can along the way, to embody humility, to stand up to bullies and show them the way to love and peace.

~—❀—~

Sometimes it doesn't take much to change a life. We give what we can and stand beside people when they need it. That's how it works. Peace.

Richard Wagamese[2]

When Donald Trump became president, we had a lot of conversations about bullying with our children. We saw a man who is a bully work his way up to become the leader of our country, and he was followed by bullies who supported him along the way. So we talked about bullying in schools, on the playground, at the park, at church, in our communities. We reminded our children that the way of loving people is never to force them. We talked about consent, about what it means to honor women, and why it's important to sit with the people that no one else pays attention to. We talked about our capacity as people to bully the earth as well.

We found that when we gave our children a little information, they knew exactly what to do. They took our words to school in how they interacted with their friends and teachers. They took our words to the market where we buy groceries from refugees who work for far too little money and are asking to be valued for who they are, not just for the work they do. They took our words to church as they watch women lead. And *they had dreams.* We believe that children are close to God, because their lives are still fresh from birth; God speaks through our children, so we listen. They have visions of a better world, and they create that world day by day. Whether we have a Democrat or a Republican in the White House, our children are the future. They will be our reality one day, and they will pass those realities on to the next generation. Can we trust them to know what they are doing? Can we trust them to stand up to systems built on the worship of bullying hate and to have honest conversations about what it means to choose love instead?

On Easter Sunday at a church we used to attend in Atlanta, all the kids come from their classes into the worship service with instruments. Little drums, tambourines, and shakers all celebrating that Jesus has destroyed death. While I question what they're being taught in church and whether they are given space to ask questions, I appreciate seeing their joy, not a joy based on acquiring salvation but a joy in knowing they are sacred, they are loved, and they belong. When I don't really know what I believe about the world, about God, about who Jesus really is in the mess we've made of history, I look at the kids. If we aren't careful, they can grow up to be like Trump, people who pervert justice and hold out their hands only to those with power. But if we let them show us the world *they see*, a world diverse and full of the mysteries of God, even our adult lives can change, and we can learn to be better people in the process.

What if all along, the story of the turtle and Original Man, the story of the muskrat diving to the bottom of the water to pull up dirt, the story of land growing where we'd least expect it—what if that's the whole point? What if the whole point is that growth comes when we least expect it, and we return to the same sacredness we are born from?

The point is that while we are here, Mystery asks us to set aside what disrupts our humanity and belonging for the chance to see what is good and to fix the things that have been broken by hate.

As we go, let's pray into the world what we believe is possible.

Prayer is only a whisper
of what could be,
what is,
the memory
of what was yesterday,
ten minutes ago,
when we last blinked and realized
that what You are
is something we cannot grasp,
but long to know
in the depths of us.
Make room,
for we are simply beginning,
the sprout that will grow
and form the landscape of tomorrow.
Breathe on us, we pray.
Iw, Amen.

PART 5 SUMMARY

What if all of this, the whole journey, the beginning, the searching, the knowing, the working, the fruit that comes from the work—what if it is all the work of knowing and being known?

What if, at the beginning and at the end of everything, the only thing that matters is that we saw and called it good—called each other good, called this kind earth good, and called the very nakedness that comes with knowing ourselves good?

Maybe, just maybe, that's the whole point of beginning again.

Maybe, just maybe, that's what the promise of a new world will always bring us.

Afterword

A FEW DAYS BEFORE I completed the manuscript of this book, I went to a local Irish pub for fish and chips, one of my favorite meals in our city. That morning, I was sitting with the heaviness of my friend Rachel Held Evans being in the hospital in an induced coma. I was sitting with the heaviness of the world, and as I wrote the words in this book, I wondered what they might do once they left my body. Words are powerful tools, and I believe we don't use them in a vacuum. What we do with words connects us to all the creatures, human and nonhuman alike, around us. My hope is that these words reach across dividing lines to say that there is a better way.

One of the most anxiety-ridden realities of writing a book is that these words are trapped in time. As I write, you are getting the Kaitlin of her thirtieth year of life, the one who has only learned as much as she can by this point. By this time next year, she will know new things, and those things will shape her. She will have found better ways to express love, better language to fight hate, and will have learned more from the books that have yet to be written by others in the world doing extraordinary work.

What you get right now is me, and I pray that as I grow, you hold that space with me, and that as you grow, I hold that space with you. May we look back on our long-ago selves with kindness and know that there were always things we should have done better.

I can't wait to see where this journey takes us—together.

Acknowledgments

OUR LIFE EXISTS both in solitude and in community, and I was able to lean into this work because of the spaces and the people who have supported me along the way. First, I give thanks to the land I currently live on, home to the Muscogee Creek and Cherokee people. I acknowledge that I am a guest here and that the history of this place, history of resilience and trauma, helps me understand my own story better. *Migwetch.*

I give thanks for the house that we moved into one year ago, thanks to generous friends who offered it to us so that I could write my books and my partner could do his research in a place of peace. I wrote so much of this book from my attic office, on long mornings with lots of coffee and a candle or two to light my way. The hawks above us reminded me to keep going no matter what. Dan and Kristin, you have given us so much here and your generosity is humbling. *Migwetch.*

Though writing this book has been difficult at times, I have known the safety of my family, that Travis, Eliot, Isaiah, and our dogs, Sam and Jupiter, will always hold space with me and remind me that I am beloved and I belong.

My family stories have made me who I am, and for that, I hold gratitude. To Mom, Steve, Tiff, Tyler, and Dad, thank you for loving me along the way.

My Indigenous kin, my Anishinaabe friends and family, have so generously supported me along the way, even as these conversations are difficult to have. I am so grateful that I get to learn from all of you and that we get to journey together as we consider what decolonization might look like for us. *Migwetch.*

Publishing a book on Indigenous spirituality and tension within the church is an intense endeavor in the world of Christian publishing. When I began this journey with Brazos, I was nervous that I wouldn't be understood or heard, and that hasn't been the case. My words and ideas and experiences have been welcomed and held with such care. To the team at Brazos, I am so grateful to work with you. Thank you for believing in this book and in my voice so that, together, we can have a difficult but necessary conversation.

In a world that is loud with Twitter chatter and Facebook rants, the quiet moments of texting with a friend or receiving and giving encouragement are rare and precious. To the friends in my writing community, thank you for holding this space with me, for grieving with me in the loss of Rachel, for reminding me that my voice matters. Jeff, Tuhina, Rachel, Nadia, Sarah, Jess, Amena, Nick, Mirabai, Mickey, Rob, Kate, Jen, Andre, Ashley, Mike, Wil, Osheta, Theresa, Meredith, Garreth, Gabes, Daniel, Prop, Brian, Wil, Audrey, Addye, Diana, Rachael, Lisa, Richard, Darryl, Melaney, Danya, Carolina, Sandra, and so many others, *migwetch.*

The moments of receiving endorsements for a book you pour yourself into can be so stressful, and yet I have been overwhelmed with gratitude again and again for the people who chose to read my words early and give their own thoughts and support. You are my partners in this work.

Self-care in the writing process of this book has been so necessary and essential. To my therapist, who reminded me along the way that I can do this and that my voice matters, your support means so much to me. I will forever be grateful for people who pour into others and encourage us to face our grief, name it, and let it work its way out in us. You are teaching us how to be brave and how to come to terms with our beautiful, sometimes terribly painful, humanity. *Migwetch*.

As I began a writing career, I had no idea how it would work. I jumped in by myself, published a book, and slowly began to find people along the way who would help me figure out what's next. To my agents, Rachelle and Jim, thank you for continuing to propel my career forward, for looking ahead to what might be on the horizon and for trusting me as I figure this out for myself as well. I am so grateful to have you on my team.

Someone recently asked me on Twitter how we are to know which parts of our life to publicly share and which parts to hold privately for ourselves and for the people we love. I answered that, often, we have a sort of gut feeling that lets us know what to share and how to set boundaries around what is public and what is private. This book is full of my life experiences, my stories, but I know they aren't just for me. They are for you, my readers, to take with you, to help you ask questions of your own stories. They are my gift to you so that you know you aren't journeying alone. Thank you for reading my words and supporting my journey.

And finally, to the continual, cyclical, complicated but precious journey of asking questions, *migwetch*. We do this because we are human, because we are dust-to-dust, and since there is no way to ask a question wrong, let us lean in and hold space with ourselves and one another.

Notes

Part 1: Beginnings

1. All poetry not otherwise attributed belongs to the author.

Chapter 1 Land and Water

1. Robin Wall Kimmerer, *Braiding Sweetgrass: Indigenous Wisdom, Scientific Knowledge, and the Teaching of Plants* (Minneapolis: Milkweed Editions, 2013), 31.

2. Lisa Dougan, "Seeking the Fourth Path," in *Oneing: An Alternative Orthodoxy* (Albuquerque: Center for Action and Contemplation, 2015), 2:66.

Chapter 2 Journeying Stories

1. Nick Estes, *Our History Is the Future* (Brooklyn: Verso, 2019), 173–74.

2. Austin Channing Brown, *I'm Still Here: Black Dignity in a World Made for Whiteness* (New York: Convergent Books, 2018), 39.

3. Mirabai Starr, *Wild Mercy: Living the Fierce and Tender Wisdom of the Women Mystics* (Boulder, CO: Sounds True, 2019).

4. Richard Rohr, *The Universal Christ: How a Forgotten Reality Can Change Everything We See, Hope For, and Believe* (New York: Convergent Books, 2019), 17.

Chapter 3 Creation Stories

1. Roxanne Dunbar-Ortiz, *An Indigenous Peoples' History of the United States* (Boston: Beacon, 2014), 1.

2. Basil Johnston, *The Manitous: The Supernatural World of the Ojibway* (New York: HarperCollins, 1995), 2–3.

3. Robin Wall Kimmerer, *Braiding Sweetgrass: Indigenous Wisdom, Scientific Knowledge, and the Teaching of Plants* (Minneapolis: Milkweed Editions, 2013), 4.

4. "Excerpts from the Letters of John Tipton," Kansas Heritage Group, 1998, http://www.kansasheritage.org/PBP/history/tipton.html.

5. Jon Boursaw, "The Flint Hills: A Major Chapter in Potawatomi Migration," *Symphony in the Flint Hills Field Journal*, https://newprairiepress.org /cgi/viewcontent.cgi?referer=https://www.google.com/&httpsredir=1&arti cle=1032&context=sfh.

6. Rachel Held Evans, *Inspired: Slaying Giants, Walking on Water, and Loving the Bible Again* (Nashville: Nelson, 2018), 16.

7. Peter Wohlleben, *The Hidden Life of Trees: What They Feel, How They Communicate—Discoveries from a Secret World* (Vancouver: Greystone Books, 2015), 17.

8. Vine Deloria Jr., *God Is Red: A Native View of Religion* (Golden, CO: Fulcrum, 2003), 87.

9. "Native Land Digital," www.native-land.ca.

10. Leanne Betasamosake Simpson, *As We Have Always Done: Indigenous Freedom through Radical Resistance* (Minneapolis: University of Minnesota Press, 2017), 154.

Chapter 4 My Own Beginning

1. Randy Woodley, *Shalom and the Community of Creation: An Indigenous Vision* (Grand Rapids: Eerdmans, 2012), xix.

2. Lisa Sharon Harper, *The Very Good Gospel: How Everything Wrong Can Be Made Right* (New York: WaterBrook, 2016), 146.

Chapter 5 The Problem of Whiteness

1. Vine Deloria Jr., *God Is Red: A Native View of Religion* (Golden, CO: Fulcrum, 2003), 68.

2. Richard Twiss, *One Church, Many Tribes: Following Jesus the Way God Made You* (Bloomington, MN: Chosen Books, 2000), 49.

3. Daniel Heath Justice, *Why Indigenous Literatures Matter* (Ontario: Wilfrid Laurier University Press, 2018), 86.

4. Kim Tallbear, *Native American DNA: Tribal Belonging and the False Promise of Genetic Science* (Minneapolis: University of Minnesota Press, 2013), 32.

5. Donald Trump, Twitter, February 9, 2019, https://twitter.com/real DonaldTrump/status/1094368870415110145.

6. Jonathan Wilson-Hartgrove, *Reconstructing the Gospel: Finding Freedom from Slaveholder Religion* (Downers Grove, IL: IVP Books, 2018), 70.

Chapter 6 Stereotypes and Survival

1. Amy B. Wang, "A Teacher Called a Native American Teen a 'Bloody Indian' and Cut Another's Braid, Students Say," *Washington Post*, December 4, 2018, https://www.washingtonpost.com/education/2018/12/04/teacher -called-native-american-teen-bloody-indian-cut-anothers-braid-students-say.

2. Daniel Heath Justice, *Why Indigenous Literatures Matter* (Ontario: Wilfrid Laurier University Press, 2018), 56.

3. Erik Brady, "Redface, Like Blackface, Is a Sin of White Supremacy," *The Undefeated*, February 25, 2019, https://theundefeated.com/features /redface-like-blackface-is-a-sin-of-white-supremacy.

4. "Tribal Nations and the United States: An Introduction," National Congress of American Indians, http://www.ncai.org/about-tribes.

Chapter 7 A Heart Language

1. Charla Bear, "American Indian Boarding Schools Haunt Many," NPR, May 12, 2018, https://www.npr.org/templates/story/story.php?storyId=16 516865.

2. Robin Wall Kimmerer, *Braiding Sweetgrass: Indigenous Wisdom, Scientific Knowledge, and the Teaching of Plants* (Minneapolis: Milkweed Editions, 2013), 53.

3. Richard Wagamese, *One Story, One Song* (Vancouver: Douglas & McIntyre, 2011), 2.

4. Roxanne Dunbar-Ortiz and Dina Gilio-Whitaker, *"All the Real Indians Died Off": And 20 Other Myths about Native Americans* (Boston: Beacon, 2016), 1–6.

Chapter 8 Gifts of Prayer

1. Jemar Tisby, *The Color of Compromise: The Truth about the American Church's Complicity in Racism* (Grand Rapids: Zondervan, 2019), 20.

2. Tommy Orange, *There, There: A Novel* (New York: Knopf, 2018), 11.

Chapter 9 Ceremony

1. "38th Trinity Institute National Theological Conference Interview with James Cone," YouTube.com, January 2008, https://www.youtube.com/watch ?v=a7NKXlmRvWE.

Chapter 10 Ancestors

1. Emmanuel Katongole and Chris Rice, *Reconciling All Things: A Christian Vision for Justice, Peace, and Healing* (Downers Grove, IL: IVP Books, 2008), 31.

2. Abraham Joshua Heschel, *I Asked for Wonder: A Spiritual Anthology* (New York: Crossroad, 1983), 45.

Chapter 11 Self, Examined

1. "Indian Country Demographics," National Congress of American Indians, 2019, http://www.ncai.org/about-tribes/demographics.

2. Frederick Buechner, *Beyond Words: Daily Readings in the ABCs of Faith* (New York: HarperOne, 2004), 139.

Chapter 12 The Pain of Church Spaces

1. Thich Nhat Hanh, *Living Buddha, Living Christ* (New York: Riverhead Books, 1995), 2.

2. Richard Rohr, *The Universal Christ: How a Forgotten Reality Can Change Everything We See, Hope For, and Believe* (New York: Convergent Books, 2019), 59.

3. Barbara A. Holmes, "Contemplating Anger," in *Oneing: An Alternative Orthodoxy* (Albuquerque: Center for Action and Contemplation, 2018), 1:23.

4. Glennon Doyle and Abby Wambach, "Un-Becoming," *On Being* (radio broadcast), interview with Krista Tippett, January 28, 2019, https://onbeing.org/programs/glennon-doyle-and-abby-wambach-un-becoming-jan2019.

5. Leanne Betasamosake Simpson, *As We Have Always Done: Indigenous Freedom through Radical Resistance* (Minneapolis: University of Minnesota Press, 2017), 52 (emphasis original).

6. Simpson, *As We Have Always Done*, 52.

7. Nick Estes, *Our History Is the Future* (Brooklyn: Verso, 2019), 79.

Chapter 13 Wake-Up Calls

1. Nick Estes, *Our History Is the Future* (Brooklyn: Verso, 2019), 248.

2. Estes, *Our History Is the Future*, 249.

3. Estes, *Our History Is the Future*, 256.

4. Richard Wagamese, *One Story, One Song* (Vancouver: Douglas & McIntyre, 2011), 35.

5. "The Six Most Dangerous Types of Activism," Amnesty International UK, May 1, 2018, https://www.amnesty.org.uk/most-dangerous-activism.

Chapter 14 When the Church Gets to Work

1. Elise Hansen, "The Forgotten Minority in Police Shootings," CNN, November 13, 2017, https://www.cnn.com/2017/11/10/us/native-lives-matter/index.html.

Chapter 15 Keeping Watch

1. Brené Brown, *Rising Strong: How the Ability to Reset Transforms the Way We Live, Love, Parent, and Lead* (New York: Penguin, 2015), 108.
2. Thomas Merton, *Seeds*, ed. Robert Inchausti (Boston: Shambhala, 2002), 34.

Chapter 16 Fighting Invisibility

1. Daniel Heath Justice, *Why Indigenous Literatures Matter* (Ontario: Wilfrid Laurier University Press, 2018), 115 (emphasis original).
2. Jean Dennison, *Colonial Entanglement: Constituting a Twenty-First-Century Osage Nation* (Chapel Hill: University of North Carolina Press, 2012), 147.
3. Andrew Clark, "Read Mike Pence's Speech from the NRA Convention in Indianapolis," *IndyStar*, April 26, 2019, https://www.indystar.com /story/news/politics/2019/04/26/mike-pence-nra-convention-indianapolis /3588784002.

Chapter 17 Finding One Another

1. Kimberlé Crenshaw, "The Urgency of Intersectionality," TED, October 2016, https://www.ted.com/talks/kimberle_crenshaw_the_urgency_of_inter sectionality. The following quotations are from this TED talk.
2. Leanne Betasamosake Simpson, *As We Have Always Done: Indigenous Freedom through Radical Resistance* (Minneapolis: University of Minnesota Press, 2017), 66.
3. Devlin Barrett, "Hate Crimes Rose 17 Percent Last Year, according to New FBI Data," *Washington Post*, November 13, 2018, https://www.washing tonpost.com/world/national-security/hate-crimes-rose-17-percent-last-year -according-to-new-fbi-data/2018/11/13/e0dcf13e-e754-11e8-b8dc-66cca4 09c180_story.html.
4. Arjun Singh Sethi, *American Hate: Survivors Speak Out* (New York: New Press, 2018), 9.
5. Krista Tippett, "Good Conversation Is an Adventure," *On Being* (radio broadcast), July 13, 2018, https://onbeing.org/blog/krista-tippett-good-con versation-is-an-adventure.

Chapter 18 The Future of Decolonization

1. Carolina Hinojosa-Cisneros, "We Survive by Telling Stories," *On Being* (radio broadcast), May 14, 2018, https://onbeing.org/blog/carolina-hinojosa -cisneros-we-survive-by-telling-stories.
2. Yaron Steinbuch, "Native American Activist Nathan Phillips Has Criminal Record," *New York Post*, January 24, 2019, https://nypost.com/2019 /01/24/native-american-activist-nathan-phillips-has-a-criminal-record.

3. Jason Le Miere, "Donald Trump Says 'Our Ancestors Tamed a Continent' and 'We Are Not Going to Apologize for America,'" *Newsweek*, May 25, 2018, https://www.newsweek.com/donald-trump-tame-continent-america-945121.

Chapter 19 Returning

1. Richard Rohr, *Simplicity: The Freedom of Letting Go* (New York: Crossroad, 1991), 25.

2. Rachel Held Evans, *Inspired: Slaying Giants, Walking on Water, and Loving the Bible Again* (Nashville: Nelson, 2018), 129.

Chapter 20 A New World for Our Children

1. Richard Rohr, *Simplicity: The Freedom of Letting Go* (New York: Crossroad, 1991), 76.

2. Richard Wagamese, *One Story, One Song* (Vancouver: Douglas & McIntyre, 2011), 84.